Interest Rates and Asset Values

In the complex world of corporate strategy and market dynamics, very few questions are as fundamental as understanding what drives the value of business assets. This book presents the first comprehensive empirical analysis of the causal relationship between interest rates and asset values in closed markets, using the unique example of the UK retail pharmacy sector, a market closed by regulation for over three decades.

It uncovers a near-perfect inverse relationship between interest rates and asset values that has persisted across multiple economic cycles, pandemics, changes of government and fundamental changes in both healthcare policy and monetary policy and offers robust proof of an economic principle long theorised but never previously demonstrated so clearly in practice. The book bridges macroeconomic theory, Keynes, Monetarism, Fisher Effect, business strategy and applied policy and offers insights relevant to economists, policymakers, business professionals and anyone interested in asset valuation in regulated markets. Original contributions include the empirical proof of the interest rate – asset value link in a genuinely closed market and the introduction of the concept of "quasi-real assets", a term that has rarely been used. This book turns it into a term which can be more usefully, and regularly, applied in economic debate.

While the book presents a UK case study, the principles and findings are applicable to any regulated or closed market worldwide and are particularly relevant to sectors like taxis, medical practices, broadcasting, etc. The book will appeal to researchers, scholars and advanced students in economics, business, finance and public policy, as well as policymakers, regulators, professional valuers and consultants.

Richard Thomas is a professor at the Swiss School of Business Research, Zurich, Switzerland.

Routledge Focus on Economics and Finance

The fields of economics are constantly expanding and evolving. This growth presents challenges for readers trying to keep up with the latest important insights. Routledge Focus on Economics and Finance presents short books on the latest big topics, linking in with the most cutting-edge economics research.

Individually, each title in the series provides coverage of a key academic topic, whilst collectively the series forms a comprehensive collection across the whole spectrum of economics.

Proactivity in Economics
Between Resourcefulness and Entrepreneurship
Jakub Bożydar Wiśniewski

The Geoeconomics of Global Value Chains
Navigating Geopolitical Complexity and Industrial Policy Shifts
Katarzyna Mroczek-Dąbrowska

Dollar Dominance
Fundamentals, Nature and Present Structure
Junji Tokunaga

Resilient Global Supply Chains and Geopolitical Risk
Evidence from Central and Eastern Europe
Aleksandra Kania

Interest Rates and Asset Values
A Case Study in Closed Markets
Richard Thomas

For more information about this series, please visit: www.routledge.com/Routledge-Focus-on-Economics-and-Finance/book-series/RFEF

Interest Rates and Asset Values

A Case Study in Closed Markets

Richard Thomas

Routledge
Taylor & Francis Group
LONDON AND NEW YORK

First published 2026
by Routledge
4 Park Square, Milton Park, Abingdon, Oxon OX14 4RN

and by Routledge
605 Third Avenue, New York, NY 10158

Routledge is an imprint of the Taylor & Francis Group, an informa business

British Library Cataloguing-in-Publication Data
A catalogue record for this book is available from the British Library

ISBN: 978-1-041-34196-3 (hbk)
ISBN: 978-1-041-34197-0 (pbk)
ISBN: 978-1-003-79155-3 (ebk)

DOI: 10.4324/9781003791553

Typeset in Times New Roman
by KnowledgeWorks Global Ltd.

Contents

Preface: The £1 Million Conundrum (and Jane Austen)

In November 2017, a small pharmacy in Oxfordshire, England, was sold for £1.25 million. By March 2024, a very similar pharmacy just five miles up the road sold for £470,000. They both had a similar customer base, similar prescription volumes, identical NHS contracts and almost the same over-the-counter trade. So why is there such a massive difference in value?

The full answer will be revealed in the forthcoming pages.

All we need to say at this stage is that there was only one meaningful difference between the two transactions. That was that the Bank of England base rate had risen from 0.5% to 5.25% in the intervening period. There were also clear signals from the Bank and the bond markets that further rises in interest rates could be expected.

This stark contrast in the value of an asset represents more than just market volatility. It reveals a fundamental relationship between interest rates and asset values that operates with mathematical precision in closed markets yet remains largely unrecognised in mainstream business strategy and financial theory.

For the course of over 32 years, from May 1993 to October 2025, I have tracked 390 pharmacy business transfer transactions (one each month) across Great Britain, documenting their sale prices as a multiple of their profit, alongside the interest rate at the time of the sale. The pattern that emerges challenges much conventional wisdom about asset pricing and offers profound implications for business strategy, investment decisions and economic policy.

The UK retail pharmacy sector provides a perfect laboratory for studying this relationship. Strict regulatory barriers limit new entrants, NHS contracts guarantee steady cash flows as well as protection from new entrants to the market, and standardised business models enable direct comparison across all the transactions recorded. Unlike most industries where variables proliferate and make analysis difficult, the controlled environment of UK retail pharmacy strips away all those other factors which can affect the supply of fixed assets to reveal the underlying truth. That is an almost completely linear inverse relationship between interest rates and business values that has persisted across more than three decades, multiple economic cycles, pandemics, changes of government and fundamental changes in both healthcare policy and monetary policy.

Despite the fact that there is a lot of discussion of Keynesianism, Monetarism and even more on integration, mergers and acquisitions, this is a book primarily about interest rates and asset values, with the key findings shown graphically at the end.

The work follows on from the excellent studies by Professor Joseph Gyourko, who works at the Wharton School of the University of Pennsylvania. He has examined how interest rate levels affect asset values in the housing market (Gyourko, 2009, pp. 375–382). This book takes the study of interest rates and asset values forward from Gyourko's work by looking at the effects of interest rate changes on an effectively closed market, where the other influences of price which affect asset values are absent. This is apparent in the case of, for example, the housing market, where building more houses can have as much influence on asset values (by increasing supply relevant to demand) as current interest rates (Gyourko, 2009).

Likewise, Shiller (1991) looks at housing prices and interest rates. He emphasises that, while housing prices are influenced by interest rates, the complete relationship is much more complex. He suggests other factors, such as speculation, psychological factors and future expectations, are also at play in determining housing values. While Shiller's work is important, it doesn't look at markets where all other determinants are stripped out, which is what this book does. His brilliant anticipation of the 2008 banking crisis (Shiller, 2007) was again based on asset values NOT moving in line with interest rates, so proving how vital that link actually is – which is the normal relationship proved here.

Again, Fama has done some important work on interest rates. But much of his work relates to financial assets (rather than the quasi-real assets this book studies). This includes his work on the capital asset pricing model (CAPM) (Fama & MacBeth, 1973), risk in financial assets (Fama & French, 1993) and his further work on the CAPM (Fama & French, 2004). These are all important works, but the assets involved are financial rather than real (as in Shiller's case) or quasi-real (as in this book).

In the same vein, Sims' work on interest rates is groundbreaking. However, his work (Sims, 1980) and (Sims, 1992) really concentrates on the effect of interest rates in terms of inflation and monetary policy, rather than their effect on asset values.

Finally, Hansen has done work in the field of interest rates. His work on GMM (Hansen, 1982) is interesting and valuable, but in the context of econometrics. It provides no empirical evidence of the link between interest rates and real or quasi-real assets. Likewise, his work on the Hansen-Singleton model is more in the realm of statistical modelling in the econometric model than a full analysis of the relationship between asset values and interest rates.

This work takes a very broad view of interest rates and their effect on wealth, including quoting Jane Austen (yes, the romantic author, Jane Austen!). We shall see in Chapter 2 whether she herself was actually an economist.

The book also clarifies a term that has rarely been used. That is the phrase 'quasi-real assets'. This book turns it into a term which can be more usefully, and regularly, applied in economic debate. I have provided a slightly altered definition, outlined below, in the section 'Empirical Evidence From Fixed Asset Values in Closed or Restricted Markets'.

So, having looked at several authors' work in the context of interest rates and asset values, it is easy to conclude that this book is groundbreaking and an advance in the theory of interest rates in three areas. Firstly, it redefines quasi-real assets in a meaningful way. Secondly, it looks at actual values of quasi-real assets in a closed market with no outside factors affecting the value of those assets. Finally, it is a long-term study of the relationship between asset prices and interest rates (where those are the only two variables), which proves Keynes' theory on the Modus Operandi of Bank Rate.

1 Introduction

The Central Question

In the complex world of corporate strategy and market dynamics, very few questions are as fundamental as understanding what drives the value of business assets. This book addresses a deceptively simple question. That is, in markets with significant barriers to entry – markets that economists term "closed markets" – what really determines the price businesses command when they change hands (i.e., what is the true value of any business)?

The answer, as this book demonstrates, reveals a remarkably clear relationship between interest rates and asset values that has profound implications for our understanding of market behaviour, corporate finance and investment strategy. Using over 32 years of business sales data from the UK retail pharmacy sector, this book provides empirical evidence for a hypothesis that challenges conventional wisdom about asset valuation in closed markets.

The central proposition is whether, in a closed, or effectively closed, market, asset prices move proportionately and inversely with interest rate movements. When interest rates fall, asset values rise by a corresponding amount. When rates rise, values fall accordingly. This relationship does not merely show a correlation but represents a fundamental economic principle operating in markets where competitive entry is restricted. While this relationship has long been assumed, carrying out research in an effectively closed market provides the empirical evidence for the relationship. This moves forward from Gyourko (2009) and Gyourko and Molloy (2015) in that we are looking here at a closed market, where the only external factor on values and prices of assets is the prevailing interest rate.

A Closed Market, or A Closed Market?

We will be examining closed markets to determine whether interest rates are the driving force on asset values. By looking at closed markets, we eliminate all other potential factors driving asset prices.

This will all be examined in later chapters.

DOI: 10.4324/9781003791553-1

However, it must be pointed out here that markets can become closed for several reasons, which will all be looked at.

The crucial point to be made at this early stage is that market closure can arise out of integration issues (see the chapters on vertical integration, disintegration, vertical control and franchising) or through regulation and licencing issues (see Chapter 7 on the regulatory closure of the UK retail pharmacy market).

Both theories lead to closed markets, which provide the ideal seedbed for examining the effect of interest rates on asset values in the context of a perfect set of data.

Market Structure and Asset Valuation

Traditional financial theory suggests that asset values reflect the discounted present value of future cash flows, adjusted for risk. While this principle holds broadly, it fails to capture the full dynamics that operate in markets where there are regulatory barriers, licensing requirements or any other structural impediments that limit market entry. In such markets, the scarcity value of operating licences, permits or any other barrier to entry becomes a significant component of the value of a business. This scarcity premium responds directly to changes in the cost of capital (specifically interest rates).

The UK retail pharmacy market provides an ideal laboratory for testing this hypothesis. Since 1988, the UK government has operated a control of entry system that effectively limits the number of pharmacies that can operate under UK National Health Service (NHS) contracts. This regulatory framework creates an effectively closed market where existing operators enjoy a form of monopolistic protection and where new entrants face substantial barriers to establishing a new business in competition. Whilst effectively protecting existing businesses from new entrants to the market, the NHS, as we shall see later, does control absolute profits by setting target operating margins on drug sales to the NHS, as well as controlling fees paid for services provided.

Unlike truly free markets where increased profitability attracts new competitors who drive down returns to competitive levels, closed markets maintain artificial scarcity. In such environments, the primary variable that affects business values becomes the discount rate applied to expected returns. This directly correlates with prevailing interest rates.

The UK Retail Pharmacy Sector as a Case Study

The choice of the UK retail pharmacy sector for this analysis was not arbitrary. This particular market exhibits several characteristics that make it particularly suitable for testing the interest rate to asset value hypothesis.

There are effectively five features which make it an appropriate model. These are listed here.

Regulatory Protection

The control of entry regulations, administered by NHS England and its predecessor organisations, creates genuine barriers to competition. New pharmacy contracts are granted only where the authorities determine that existing provision is inadequate. This is a test that has proven stringent since its introduction.

Although new pharmacy contracts are granted, effectively they must be in an area not directly served by an existing pharmacy.

Standardised Revenue Streams

The overwhelming majority of pharmacy revenue (over 90% in recent years) derives from the NHS contract with pharmacies. This has standardised fee structures and a cap on overall profit margins obtainable from drug dispensing on behalf of the NHS. This reduces the variability in income streams that might otherwise complicate valuation analysis.

Active Transaction Market

Despite the regulatory constraints (or perhaps because of them), pharmacy businesses in the UK change hands regularly, creating a robust and long-term dataset of transaction prices which give good financial performance metrics.

Long-Term Data Availability

The research benefits from over three decades of transaction data. I have collected detailed data over a period of more than 32 years. This data spans multiple interest rate cycles and regulatory changes.

Homogeneous Business Model

While pharmacies vary in size and location, their fundamental business model remains consistent. This is basically the standard NHS contract providing around 90% of income, with some (about 10% of turnover) counter sales. This reduces the variables that might otherwise affect comparative valuations.

This combination of factors creates what economists would recognise as a natural experiment. That is a market environment where the primary variable affecting asset values is only the cost of capital, as represented by the prevailing interest rate.

Other Closed Markets

While the market examined here is a good example of a closed market, other markets could be chosen for study.

Any market which is closed, or effectively closed, to further expansion of supply will exhibit similar dynamics in terms of the relationship of the value of the assets to interest rates.

By their nature, these markets will usually be markets in quasi real assets (which are defined later, differently from the definition used by J. M. Keynes). These markets include anything that is regulated in terms of supplying contracts. For example, taxi licences in many large cities are regulated, and new entrants to the market usually need to buy an existing licence. Also, many retail franchise operations are controlled by the franchisor in such a way that new entry into the market is virtually impossible.

Any market such as these very restricted entry markets, in any country, will exhibit the same complete relationship between the prevailing interest rate and the asset value of the businesses being examined.

Research Methodology and Data Collection

This research represents the culmination of over 32 years of primary data collection. It has been built on earlier work conducted for a master's degree and has subsequently been expanded to take account of the extended time series of data that is presented here. The methodology combines both quantitative analysis of transaction data with qualitative assessment of market conditions and regulatory changes.

Data Collection and Analysis

The data collection process was as follows.

The core dataset comprises 390 individual pharmacy business transactions where the sale was completed between May 1993 and October 2025. Each transaction record included:

1 The complete financial accounts for the business in its final full trading year before its sale.
2 The actual sale price that was achieved.
3 The date of completion of the sale.
4 The multiple of not profit that the sale price represented (the key component of the data).
5 Also noted in the data collection process were basic business characteristics. This was done to ensure there were no other external factors affecting the data collected. These characteristics included the location, size, ownership structure and any other relevant facts.

There are a few transactions where these factors have affected the sale price of the business, and where this has happened, that is noted.

Confidentiality and Access

All data has been collected under strict confidentiality agreements with business transfer agents, lending institutions and market participants. While the specific identity of individual businesses cannot be disclosed, the anonymised data (composed of items 1–4 above, but excluding the background data in item 5) provides a complete picture of market activity across the research period. I have a datasheet (password protected) of all the information in item 5, which might identify a business or its buyer and seller.

Representativeness

The dataset represents approximately 40–50% of all pharmacy transactions during the study period. The sample is not systematically biased towards any particular size, location or ownership category. As such, it provides a representative cross section of market activity during the period.

Data Standardisation

To enable meaningful comparison across different accounting practices and time periods, all financial data (the accounts) has been standardised using consistent definitions and methodologies. This includes adjusting for the costs of an owner-manager (where this is not shown in self-employed or owner-managed business accounts), dealing with rental versus freehold considerations (putting a notional rent into the accounts where there is a freehold owned) and stripping out financing expenses.

Analytical Approach

The research in this book employs both descriptive and inferential statistical methods to examine the relationship between interest rates and asset valuations. The primary analytical framework centres on calculating profit multiples – the ratio of the transaction price to earnings before interest, tax, depreciation and amortisation (EBITDA) – for each transaction.

These multiples are then analysed against the contemporaneous Bank of England base interest rate.

This comparison of interest rates to profit multiples identifies patterns and correlations. The extended time series allows for examination of the relationship across multiple economic cycles, including periods of both rising and falling interest rates.

The key findings are brought together in four fundamental graphs at the end of the work, which graphically show the proof of the link between interest rates and asset values.

Structure of This Book

This book is organised to build systematically from the theoretical foundations of both interest rates and the closed UK retail pharmacy market, through empirical analysis to actual research findings. It also includes practical conclusions and recommendations following on from those findings.

The early chapters look at interest rate theories and go on to establish the conceptual framework for understanding vertical integration and its role in creating and maintaining closed markets. The middle chapters then examine the specific case of the UK retail pharmacy sector, while the later chapters present the empirical findings. The implications of those findings follow in an appendix.

This book throughout maintains focus on proof of the central finding while providing sufficient context to understand its significance. The relationship between interest rates and asset values in closed markets represents more than an academic curiosity. It also offers practical insights for anyone involved in valuing, buying or selling businesses in regulated industries.

The Theoretical Foundation (Chapters 2–6)

Chapter 2 looks at the literature surrounding classic interest rate theories. Chapters 3–6 review the extensive literature on vertical integration, examining why firms choose to integrate, the various forms integration can take, and the circumstances that lead to disintegration. The theoretical grounding in both interest rates and integration is essential for understanding how prices in closed markets develop. Taken together, these five chapters marry together the theory of the market I am examining with the theory of the interest rates which affect that market.

Analysis of Case Studies (Chapters 7 and 8)

The focus shifts to the UK retail pharmacy sector, examining its regulatory structure, supply chain characteristics and the specific forms of vertical integration and control that have emerged. This analysis demonstrates how regulatory barriers create the closed market conditions necessary for testing the interest rate hypothesis.

Empirical Evidence Proving the Theory (Chapter 9)

The heart of the book presents the transaction data and statistical analysis that supports the central hypothesis. This chapter also looks at the way in which the data was collected, analysed, presented and interpreted.

It also suggests ways in which, if thought necessary, the data could be reanalysed to rule out anomalous findings.

The Absolute Proof That Interest Rates Drive Asset Values (Chapter 10)

This chapter is the key to both the whole book and to the study of interest rates overall. It clearly demonstrates the remarkably consistent relationship between interest rates and asset values. It does this across a research timescale of more than three decades of market activity.

As such, it provides definitive proof of Keynes' theory on the Modus Operandi of Bank Rate in relation to quasi-real assets (which are defined slightly differently here to differentiate from the more financial assets that Keynes had in mind).

Implications for Policy Makers, Businesses and Economic Theory (Appendix D)

This is put as an appendix to the book, as it does not form part of the actual empirical proof of the theory, which is so central to the interest rate and asset value relationship (although as the implications do fall out of the findings, it is included for the sake of completeness). The appendix explores what these findings mean for investors, business people, policymakers and academic economists. It also suggests possible directions for future research.

2 Classic Interest Rate and Monetarism Theory

An In-Depth Overview

Classic interest rate theory and monetarism represent the two fundamental schools of thought in economics, particularly in the fields of macroeconomic policy, interest rates, monetary dynamics and the functioning of financial markets.

Classic interest rate theory deals with the determinants and implications of interest rates in an economy, while monetarism focuses on the role the money supply holds in influencing economic output and price levels.

This chapter looks at both theories, tracing their intellectual origins, development and key tenets. It critiques their place in contemporary economic thought. The important point is that it puts the interest rate aspect of this book into context so that it can be linked to the closed market for fixed assets which is examined later.

Classic Interest Rate Theory

Origins and Foundations

Classic interest rate theory has its roots in the works of the earliest economists, such as Adam Smith, David Ricardo and John Stuart Mill (Mill, 1848; Ricardo, 1817 and Smith, 1776). The classical school viewed interest as the price that borrowers paid for the use of lenders' capital. They viewed it as similar to the rent paid by tenants to landlords for the right to hold and use land. They believed that interest rates (the price of money) were determined by the balance between the supply of funds to be lent and the demand for borrowing.

The Loanable Funds Theory

The loanable funds theory proposes that the interest rate is set by the equilibrium between savings (the supply of loanable funds) and investment (the demand for loan funding). In this framework, households supply funds by saving, and firms seek funds to finance investment projects. When savings

DOI: 10.4324/9781003791553-2

increase, the supply of funds rises, leading to a decrease in interest rates (if all else is equal). On the other hand, an increase in the demand for money to fund investment raises interest rates. It is a classic example of the theory of supply and demand (in this case for money itself).

Loanable funds theory incorporates both time preference (the preference that everybody naturally has for having something now – present consumption – rather than waiting – 'delayed gratification') and the productivity of capital (the expected return on an investment). The intersection of these forces determines the natural rate of interest – the rate at which the economy is at full employment without inflationary or deflationary pressures.

Critiques and Evolution

John Maynard Keynes famously critiqued the classical view, arguing that interest rates are not solely determined by savings and investment but also by liquidity preference – the demand for money as an asset (Keynes, 1936, pp. 166–174). Keynes' liquidity preference theory suggested that interest rates will adjust to equate the supply and demand for money itself, not just loanable funds. This view challenged the classical perspective, particularly during periods of economic instability or liquidity tightening. This was seen particularly during the Great Depression (which was at the time that Keynes was writing), as well as other periods since, such as after the banking crisis in 2008 and the COVID-19 pandemic of 2020–2021. It was also evident in the United Kingdom after the vote to leave the European Union in 2016 ("Brexit"). These latter periods are pertinent to parts of the study period outlined below and are so particularly consequential to the findings.

The liquidity preference theory is especially relevant during times of economic uncertainty or policy shifts, as seen in the periods following financial crises, during which traditional relationships can break down or behave in unexpected ways. Although it is interesting that in times of uncertainty and upheaval (e.g., major wars) there is often a shift away from bank deposits into real (but non-interest earning) assets such as gold.

Interest Rates and the Price of Capital – Keynes' Theory Proved

Keynes (1930, pp. 196–202) moved beyond his critique of the classical view of interest rates outlined above. He argued that the interest rate is not simply a function of the supply and demand for loanable funds. It is, critically, influenced by the public's preference for liquidity – i.e., the desire to hold cash as opposed to investments in securities or other assets. Cash is always an asset which can be used instantly, at a known value, whereas other assets may vary in value and may not be instantly realisable. This he described as the 'modus operandi' of bank rates. He stated, "The rate of interest is the price which equilibrates the desire to hold wealth in the form of cash with the available quantity of cash" (Keynes, 1930, p. 199).

Keynes's theoretical argument shows that if the public want to hold cash in interest-bearing short-term deposits, then, in order for them to invest in longer-term assets, the value of the asset must fall as interest rates rise (and vice versa).

I will show later that in markets where external factors are tightly controlled and there are barriers to entry into that market (such as, but not uniquely, the UK retail pharmacy market), the relationship between interest rates and asset values becomes unusually clear and direct. This empirically proves Keynes' theory on the modus operandi of bank rates for quasi-real assets.

This book's empirical research shows that in these closed markets, asset values move almost perfectly inversely with the prevailing interest rate – when rates fall, asset values rise and vice versa. This is perfectly demonstrated graphically in Chapter 10.

Further Developments in Interest Rate Theory

The Fisher Effect

Irving Fisher (1930, pp. 355–362) suggested that nominal interest rates reflect both the real interest rate and expected inflation. The Fisher equation is:

$$\text{Nominal interest rate} = \text{Real interest rate} + \text{Expected inflation rate}$$

This concept explains how inflation expectations become embedded in interest rates, influencing both lenders and borrowers (Fisher, 1930). Inflation has now been accounted for in many areas of economics and has lent itself to the phrase "in real terms". That is how much extra does anybody earn after a nominal rise in income (in wages or interest) after taking account of the devaluing effect on money of inflation.

Basically, the rate of interest needs to be interest plus inflation to make saving worthwhile.

This is a vital concept, as, if invested at the 'natural' rate of interest when interest rates are constantly lower than the current rate of inflation, then the value of the income will diminish. The sub-chapter on Jane Austen, below, demonstrates the point.

Term Structure of Interest Rates

The term structure, or yield curve, shows how interest rates vary with the maturity of debt. There are many elements to how the yield curve works and why interest rates vary according to the term of the debt.

There are three main key theories on the differences between long- and short-term rates.

The first is the Expectations Theory (Vasicek, 1977, pp. 177–188). This shows that long-term interest rates reflect the expected future short-term rates. So, if the one-year rate today were 4.5%, but the market expected one-year rates in 12 months' time to be 4%, then the expectations theory would say that two-year rates would currently be lower than one-year rates (at about 4.25%). There is some logic to this theory, but it seems to be overridden by other, competing theories.

The second key theory is the Liquidity Preference Theory (Keynes, 1936, pp. 166–179 and 194–198).

This states that investors demand a premium for longer maturities. There are two reasons why investors do this. Firstly, there is the time preference referred to above in the loanable funds theory, where holding cash readily available for either investment or consumption now is better than having that cash in the future. Secondly, there is a greater risk factor, in that funds lent for a longer period become inherently more likely to be defaulted on, creating a bad debt.

The third theory of long-term interest rates is the Market Segmentation Theory (Culbertson, 1957, pp. 495–498). This theory suggests that supply and demand in each maturity segment drive rates. Investors each have a preference for a different maturity. This is particularly evident with pension funds, which are keen to match the maturities of their investments to their future liabilities to pensioners. The theory states that such investors don't switch their investment maturity preferences and so always seek the same time maturity. This creates anomalies in the supply and demand for funds of different maturities, which therefore affects the price (interest rate) of individual maturities.

There is one other interesting fact about the yield curve that makes it a crucial economic indicator. Estrella and Mishkin (1996, pp. 1–9) showed that an inverted yield curve is often a predictor of recessions. They showed that many recessions had been preceded by an inverted yield curve.

Interest Rate Parity and International Finance

Interest rate parity (IRP) explains how differences in national interest rates are offset by changes in exchange rates, preventing arbitrage between countries and their currencies (Keynes, 1923, pp. 118–120).

The key element here is not so much interest rates as the exchange rate between different currencies.

An easy way of explaining IRP is through the 'Big Mac Index'. This uses the price of a McDonald's Big Mac hamburger in different countries to compare the relative value of currencies. The idea is that the same product (a Big Mac) should cost roughly the same everywhere when expressed in a common currency, according to the theory of purchase price parity (PPP).[1] If it doesn't, one currency may be over- or under-valued compared to another.

The theory is that, for example (taking two countries at random) if a Big Mac costs $5.00 in the United States and ¥400 in Japan, the implied PPP exchange rate is 400/5, so 80 Yen per dollar.

However, if the actual exchange rate is 100 Yen per dollar, then the Yen is undervalued against the dollar according to the Big Mac Index.

These differences can be both explained by and caused by a difference in interest rates in Yen and US dollars. If the interest rate on Yen is higher than the interest rate on US dollars, then investors will be encouraged to invest in Yen, pushing up the value of Yen versus the dollar, and vice versa.

Of course, this becomes a multi-dimensional calculation, as many different currencies will have different interest rates and different PPPs. Investors will have different views of the future prospects of a particular country's economy, whereby they may take the view that the price of a Big Mac in one country may fall in (currently) dollar terms (as the exchange rate in that currency falls). The important thing is the view they take of the value in what they perceive as a universal currency (at the moment US dollars, but previously in UK Sterling or Gold, in the days of the gold standard, and possibly in the future in a different currency such as Yen or Yuan).

The Zero Lower Bound and Negative Interest Rates

Traditionally, nominal interest rates were believed to have a lower bound at zero. This is despite the view that there was a natural 'real' interest rate of 2% (see r* below). However, after the 2008 crisis, central banks in Europe and Japan began to either adopt negative actual interest rates or to discuss the possibility of negative rates openly. This challenged both classical theory and traditional monetary policy (Rogoff, 2017, pp. 4–6 and 101–106).

There can be important effects on investment decisions of negative interest rates (which is the reason it was considered that they should be incorporated into monetary policy). Firms will be prepared to pay more for income-earning assets (either as a multiple of their profits or with a longer payback period) than they otherwise would have.

This occurred quite frequently during a period when investing firms expected to be charged interest for keeping cash in a bank account. It became so common that a few examples of this can be seen in the data that will be analysed later during the study period, particularly in 2016 after the UK Brexit vote.

The Natural Rate of Interest (r)*

The natural or neutral rate of interest is said to be the rate at which interest rate policy leads to neither expansion nor contraction in the economy.

This was first theorised by Wicksell (1898, pp. 102–107) and is central to modern monetary policy debates (Laubach and Williams, 2003, pp. 1063–1065).

It has long been thought that a natural rate of interest is 2% per annum. However, this is affected by the level of inflation in an economy (so affecting Fisher's 'real' rate of interest. It could alternatively be thought of as a real rate of 2%, meaning in reality 2% plus the prevailing rate of inflation).

Behavioural Perspectives on Interest Rates

Behavioural economics has shown that psychological factors influence interest rates (Shiller, 2003, pp. 105–107). These factors can influence interest rates in ways classical models may not be able to predict.

These would include risk aversion. This is quite a logical factor.

Another influencing factor is 'herding', which is often seen in the market. The theory here is that professional investors will follow the herd so as not to make a mistake by missing out (also, if the course of action goes wrong, there is the excuse that everybody else was doing it).

Policy Rate Transmission Mechanisms

Central banks' interest rate policies affect the economy directly through bank lending rates (which are always linked to the central bank lending rate). These lending rates affect exchange rates (through an avoidance of arbitrage).

The arbitrage effect is that if interest rates rise in one currency, then its value will rise unless there are other economic factors which depress that currency's value – this explains why countries with weak economic performance vis-à-vis others have a higher interest rate. If their interest rate were to be the same as those of stronger economies, then the value of their currency would fall. This explains the run on Sterling in the run-up to Black Wednesday in September 1992, when the UK government repeatedly increased interest rates to keep the level of sterling higher than markets expected it to be.

Investment, consumer spending and, as we will see in detail, asset prices are affected by central banks' interest rate policies. Understanding how these channels work is critical for assessing monetary policy effectiveness (Bernanke and Gertler, 1995, pp. 27–29 and 37–39).

The purpose of this book is not to examine those channels in detail. But it is important to be aware of the way all of them interact to be able to comprehend in their entirety the interest rate to asset value theme, which is central to this work.

Was Jane Austen Actually an Economist?

Jane Austen is such a renowned author that her credentials as a writer do not need to be mentioned.

However, from the economic perspective of interest rate theory, those credentials probably do.

Jane Austen wrote to her sister Cassandra, "I am very much obliged to my dear little George [Jane and Cassandra's brother] for his message- tell him that I hope he will always keep his money in the funds".[2]

By "the funds", she meant what were termed in those days 'consols' (loans to the UK consolidated fund), which are the equivalent of UK government bonds today.

When she wrote that letter in 1813, the yield on 3% UK government consuls was 5.2% (Homer and Sylla, 2005, p.153).[3] The 3% was the nominal rate paid on the original amount lent to the government, but the value of the consuls had fallen, leading to a rise in the yield.

The reason for the fall in the value of consuls, and the rise in their yield, was that the inflation rate in Britain in 1813 was estimated at approximately 15%.[4] This reflected the usual (see "Money Supply as a Cause of Inflation" later in this book) wartime fiscal pressures of additional government spending, increasing the money supply, and the subsequent monetary disruption.

For example, in Sense and Sensibility (Austen, 1813), the fortune left to the Dashwood sisters is presumed to have been invested in the funds, and discussions of "five percents" or "three percents" refer to the annual nominal interest paid on such government securities.[5]

In Persuasion (Austen, 1818, Chapter 17): Anne Elliot's friend Mrs Smith's income "depends on the interest of her money", which is "in the funds".

Likewise, Anne de Bourgh in Pride and Prejudice (Austen, 1813, Chapter 57) had "A very large fortune, consisting entirely of an estate in one of the northern counties and 50,000 pounds in the funds".

Of course, with an interest rate on investments of 5.2%, but an inflation rate of 15%, not only was the real value of the capital investment falling year on year, but, more importantly for those whose sole income it was, the real value of the income was falling year on year as well.

So, Jane Austen was fully aware, and shows in her writing, that interest rates were both nominal and real, and the effect that movements in those rates and inflation could have on, often meagre, incomes of distressed gentlefolk (usually women) in the early 19th century.

Piketty (2014, p. 2) picked up on the points Austen made. He notes that "Both Balzac Austen depict societies in which fortunes were often based on rents from land, government bonds, and other forms of capital, and in which the social order rested on a clear understanding of these sources of wealth".

Monetarism: The Role of Money in the Economy

The Monetarist Revival

Monetarism emerged as a response to Keynesianism in the mid-20th century. It was most prominently championed by Milton Friedman (Friedman, 1968, pp. 1–17) and was influenced by the Austrian economist Friedrich Hayek (Hayek, 1945, pp. 519–524 and 526–528; 1941, pp. 3–7 and 409–415; 1974, pp. 1–5 and 1978, pp. 183–208). While Hayek was not strictly a monetarist, his emphasis on the importance of information (Hayek, 1945), spontaneous market order (Hayek, 1974) and the dangers of central planning (Hayek, 1941 and 1945) influenced the intellectual environment that shaped the Chicago School (of which Milton Friedman was part).

Monetarists argue that the primary driver of economic activity and price levels is the money supply, rather than fiscal policy or government intervention. Importantly, inflation can be caused by an oversupply of money in an economy. This means that controlling the money supply becomes a key component in controlling inflation. This challenges the more fiscal outlook of Keynes.

The Quantity Theory of Money

The basic concept of monetarism is the Quantity Theory of Money (Friedman, 1956, pp. 4–9). This says that the general price level of goods and services is directly proportional to the amount of money in circulation. In other words, changes in the money supply have a direct, predictable effect on price levels (inflation) and economic activity (the growth rate). This work is supported by Mankiw (2021, pp. 635–641), although Mankiw does highlight the limitations of the theory and the need to take account of other factors.

This theory underpins the monetarist view that controlling the money supply is the key to managing inflation and so keeping the economy stable. It is also key to the worldwide policy (almost universal in the 21st century) of using monetary policy (i.e., Interest rates) as the key tool in controlling inflation.

The foundational concept of monetarism in the Quantity Theory of Money is often expressed as the equation MV = PY. Where:

M = Money Supply
V = Velocity of Money (frequency at which money changes hands)
P = Price Level
Y = Real Output (GDP)

Monetarists contend that, in the long run, changes in the money supply (M) lead directly to proportional changes in the price level (P), assuming velocity (V) and output (Y) are stable or predictable. This means that "inflation is always and everywhere a monetary phenomenon", according to Friedman (Friedman, 1963, pp. 17 and 676–678). Of course, changes in velocity (V) and/or output (Y) can also, therefore, affect the level of inflation, even if the money supply remains stable.

Money Supply as a Cause of Inflation

There are two classic examples of increasing money supply affecting prices when the supply side of the economy could not keep up with that increase in the money supply.

The most pertinent example was that there was a surge in inflation in Europe in the early 1500s. The precise level of inflation, as well as the actual increase in money supply, is difficult to evaluate due to the insufficient data recorded at the time (and, indeed, the accuracy of any data recorded).

Economists and historians have attributed much of the inflation in Europe at the time to the massive influx of precious metals – especially gold and silver – from the Americas. Basically, Spanish galleons came back from South America laden with gold (which at that time was the major currency). European money supply increased, according to different estimates, by between three and five times.

Despite the lack of accurate data, the phenomenon known as the 'Price Revolution' in Europe during the early 16th century has been widely documented (Cipolla, 1956, pp. 83–84). According to Cipolla, "the quantities of precious metals in circulation in Europe increased about five times between 1500 and 1650".

Niall Ferguson (Ferguson, 2008, p. 39) tells us that "the European money supply more than tripled between 1500 and 1600".

Hamilton (1934, pp. 283–284 and 325–329), in his classic early work on the subject, provides a detailed quantitative analysis of how the import of South American silver and gold contributed to rising prices (inflation), initially in Spain (it was Spanish ships largely bringing the gold to Europe), but then spreading out across Europe as a whole.

Finally, in terms of the New World gold influx, Flynn and Giráldez (1995, pp. 201–204 and 208–213) discuss the global flow of silver and its economic effects, including on European inflation.

So there is ample historical evidence (albeit not precise data) of the increased money supply causing inflationary effects, irrespective of any other factors. The increase in gold and silver supply in the early 1500s was purely due to suddenly importing a massive extra amount of gold (money) with no other changes in the existing economies of Europe.

Going back to the equation MV = PY, M increased massively, with no change in either V or Y, so for the equation to hold, there had to be a corresponding increase in P, which indeed there was.

The second example of increased money supply causing inflation is that of the funding by the US government of the Vietnam War.

There has been much discussion about global inflation in the early 1970s and how it may have been caused by the expansion of the world money supply. The US fiscal and monetary policies – partly driven by Vietnam War spending – played a significant role in this monetary expansion.

However, the link is more complex than a simple doubling of the world money supply caused solely by US war spending. Historians and economists often cite a combination of factors. These do include the loosening of US monetary policy and deficit spending (especially for the cost of the Vietnam War, but also for domestic social policies). But there was also the collapse of the Bretton Woods[6] international system at the same time, which also affected inflation. Collectively, these led to global inflation and the so-called "Great Inflation" of the 1970s. Of course, there was also the inflationary effect of the increase in oil prices imposed by OPEC in the mid-1970s.

However, Eichengreen (2008, pp. 113–123) discusses how US monetary expansion, deficit spending and the Vietnam War undermined the dollar's gold convertibility. This, it is argued, led to the collapse of the Bretton Woods system, and to a surge in global inflation. "The global inflation of the early 1970s has been attributed to the US expansionary fiscal and monetary policies, partly to finance the Vietnam War, and the subsequent collapse of the Bretton Woods system, which effectively doubled the world money supply", he states.

This argument builds on the original work by Bordo and Eichengreen (1993, pp. 3–8, 45–52 and 464–466), which originally explored the impact of US fiscal and monetary policies (including spending on the Vietnam War) on the breakdown of Bretton Woods and the subsequent worldwide inflation.

Meltzer (2005, pp. 302–315 and 348–350) and James (1996, pp. 213–220 and 224–227) also give detailed accounts of how the expansion of the US money supply and fiscal imbalances had a severe impact on world inflation during the 1970s.

In terms of war spending, there is also the inflation in the United Kingdom caused by the Napoleonic Wars, described in the section on Jane Austen in Chapter 2 above.

As a result of the adverse impact demonstrated on inflation by loose monetary (and indeed fiscal) policies, monetarists argue for predictable, rules-based monetary policy. This includes such policies as a constant money growth rate, which avoids the destabilising effects of discretionary policy interventions. Monetarists are sceptical of fiscal policy and government attempts to fine-tune the economy through deficit spending (this is often popularly termed in the United Kingdom 'the Government just prints more money'). They believe that such efforts often result in unintended consequences, including inflation or asset bubbles.

Monetarism and Interest Rates

While monetarism focuses on money supply, it does not (indeed cannot, by its nature) ignore interest rates. Monetarists view interest rates as the price of money and credit. This is influenced by central bank policies but is ultimately subordinate to the quantity of money in an economy in determining macroeconomic outcomes. They argue that attempts to set interest rates without regards to money supply can lead to cycles of boom (with inflationary pressure) and bust (with recessionary implications). They believe that since the interest rate is the price of money, demand for it can be reduced by increasing rates (the price), thereby reducing the money supply.

Critiques of Monetarism

Critics of monetarism point out that the relationship between money supply and nominal GDP is not always stable, as the velocity of money changing hands can be volatile. This is particularly true during financial crises. Further, the rise of financial innovation has complicated the measurement and control of money supply aggregates, limiting the practical utility of strict monetarist policy rules. Money can move much faster (especially in the consumer sector) now that we have electronic means of payment (and purchase through the Internet) rather than in the days when physical cash had to change hands.

Synthesis and Modern Applications

The New Consensus

In recent decades, many economists have synthesised elements of classic interest rate theory and monetarism to form the basis of modern central banking. Today's central banks, such as the Federal Reserve, the Bank of England and the European Central Bank, use interest rates and monetary aggregates (such as quantitative easing and tightening) as tools to achieve their goals of price stability and full employment. Some have specific targets to meet (the Bank of England has an inflation target of 2% set by the UK government).

The Taylor Rule and Inflation Targeting

The Taylor Rule, a widely cited guideline, suggests that central banks set short-term interest rates based on deviations of inflation from target and output from potential (Taylor, 1993, pp. 202–203 and 208–211). This approach integrates insights from both classic and monetarist traditions, recognising the interplay between money, interest rates and economic activity. Inflation targeting regimes, now common worldwide, reflect the monetarist emphasis on price stability but use interest rates as the operative policy tool.

The Enduring Debate

There is still debate between classic interest rate theory and monetarism. It continues to inform both academic and real-world policy discussions.

Key questions remain and are debated in academia and central banks around the world when the latter are setting interest rates.

The questions surround how to move the level of interest rates to control inflation, while ensuring there is not a significant deflationary (or recessionary) impact on output? Should central banks try to be ahead of the curve and move interest rates early or lag behind and try to 'play catch-up' with the rise or fall in inflationary pressures? Should central banks respond to inflationary pressures which are clearly outside the control of any interest rate policy? To what extent should central banks respond to what may turn out to be short-term shocks to the financial system? And underlying all these questions, how important or efficient is the transmission mechanism from money supply and interest rates into real economic activity?

Empirical Evidence from Fixed Asset Values in Closed or Restricted Markets

Interest Rates and Asset Values

This is a key part of this book, as the practical application of the theories set out in the research proves these theories in a way which isn't entirely possible outside a closed market, which has no external factors which influence asset prices. The research also focuses on real asset prices, rather than bonds or equities.

The assets studied are not 'real' in the sense that they are physical, but they are real in the sense that entrepreneurs do buy them in order to run a business, rather than as a financial asset – I call them 'quasi-real' assets. I do diverge from Keynes[7] on this point, in that I view quasi-real assets as concessions, long-term contracts or licences, which have a value, are necessary to business, but have no physical presence. In the UK retail pharmacy market, examined later, NHS contracts provide a goodwill value to a business. Therefore, my definition of a quasi-real asset is effectively a goodwill value, which can be bought or sold as a business asset, just as a building or a machine. Sometimes the quasi-real assets in a business are more valuable than the total of real assets. They are often shown in business accounts as 'goodwill', although this term also applies to amounts paid for a business which would not come into the category of an asset at all. This definition, while illustrated perfectly by this NHS example, is found elsewhere in various guises.

Understanding the link between interest rates and real or quasi-real asset values is critical for investors, policymakers and anyone involved in financial decision-making.

The theoretical relationship between interest rates and asset values is robust. It is strongly supported by research in open markets (Bodie, Kane and Marcus, 2021; Campbell and Shiller, 1988; Cochrane, 2005 and Mishkin, 2018).

Mishkin (2018, pp. 75–80 and 148–153) explains the inverse relationship between interest rates and asset prices, particularly for bonds and equities, and provides the theoretical foundations for chapters on asset valuation.

Bodie Kane and Marcus (2021, pp. 42–44, 415–419 and 564–566) cover the fundamental link between interest rates and the present value of future cash flows, which underpins asset valuation. This is similar to Mishkin's work, in that it is not dealing with 'real' assets. Likewise, Campbell and Shiller (1988, pp. 198–202 and 213–217) empirically examine the effect of movements in discount rates (which are closely related to interest rates) on asset prices. Finally, Cochrane (2005, pp. 13–19 and 403–408) provides a comprehensive theoretical framework for how interest and discount rates affect asset values, but again, not 'real' assets.

However, the dynamics can differ in either 'closed' or restricted markets or in the sector looked at later, a virtually closed market. That is a market where the barriers to entry are so high that new entrants either cannot or will not choose to enter. This market closure can arise from regulation, segmentation, or limited capital movement or competition. It can occur for fixed assets such as real estate and infrastructure (real assets) but is particularly found in markets where a licence or restricted contract is required for entry to the market (quasi-real assets).

Interest rates are a fundamental determinant of asset values across financial markets. There are a number of ways in which interest rates affect the value of financial assets.

The relationship is most directly observed through the process of discounting future cash flows. In terms of the present value of future incoming cash flow, the value of an asset, particularly (but not limited to) bonds or shares, is calculated as the present value of its expected future cash flows. This is discounted at a rate that reflects both the time value of money and risk, as well as the prevailing interest rate. The time value and risk cost will generally move fairly slowly. But when interest rates rise, the discount rate increases, causing the present value of future cash flows (and thus asset prices) to fall. Conversely, lower interest rates increase asset values (Brealey, Myers and Allen, 2020, pp. 21–28, 41–43 and 73–75).

In the same way, bond prices are inversely related to interest rates. When market rates rise, existing bonds with lower coupon payments become less attractive, so their prices fall. The concept of 'duration' measures a bond's sensitivity to interest rate changes (Macaulay, 1938, pp. 44–53). The classic measure of this, certainly in the United Kingdom, was War Loan 3 ½% stock. This was issued in 1917 to pay for the First World War and was effectively undated. So, the value of it moved perfectly in line with movements in interest rates over the years.[8]

When looking at shares, various stock valuation models such as the Dividend Discount Model (DDM) or Discounted Cash Flow (DCF) come into play. The discount rate used in these valuation models is usually derived from prevailing central bank interest rates. Lower interest rates tend to make equities more attractive by reducing the discount rate, boosting their valuation (Campbell and Shiller, 1988, pp. 197–202 and 213–217).

The same principle applies to real estate (land and buildings) and other long-duration assets (as well as the quasi-assets alluded to above). This principle is that lower interest rates reduce the cost of borrowing and increase the present value of future income streams. This supports higher valuations or prices (Gyourko, 2009, pp. 375–381).[9] The central thrust of this book builds on Gyourko's work by demonstrating the effect in a market with no external factors that affect the price or value of assets.

Persistently low interest rates have sometimes been linked to asset price bubbles, as cheap financing encourages speculative behaviour and higher valuations (Borio and Lowe, 2002, pp. 2–3 and 22–29). This is demonstrated in the effect of the ultra-low UK (and worldwide) interest rate levels following the banking crisis of 2008. Asset prices in the data studied did not fall until interest rates rose, with a near-perfect correlation of rates to asset values. Whether or not that can be described as an asset price bubble is debatable. Asset bubbles tend to occur in financial assets rather than real or quasi-real assets. With the latter, there is always an income-earning potential, which will allow for the payment of interest. The issue will only occur if and when interest rates rise rapidly and unexpectedly, outpacing the earning capacity of the underlying asset.

A substantial body of research works towards demonstrating the empirical link between interest rates and real asset prices in open markets. Comprehensive reviews by Gyourko (2009, pp. 375–381) and Gyourko and Molloy (2015, pp. 1290–1294 and 1327–1330)[10] bring together a wide range of studies. These highlight a strong consensus that lower interest rates are associated with higher asset prices across housing and real estate markets. While these reviews themselves do not present new empirical tests, they document the breadth and strength of evidence in the field. For direct empirical analysis, Borio and Lowe (2002, pp. 22–29) examine international data and statistically show that periods of low interest rates are often accompanied by rising real asset values and the potential for financial imbalances. Thus, both the survey literature and original empirical studies provide strong support for the relationship between interest rates and asset values. This work (along with Gyourko's) goes further in absolutely proving the link by examining a virtually closed market with no external drivers.

The downside of much existing research is that the extent to which interest rates influence asset prices, particularly in housing markets, depends critically on the supply side. As Gyourko (2009, pp. 381–389) and Gyourko and Molloy (2015, pp. 1306–1310 and 1327–1330) emphasise, in markets where housing supply is flexible and responsive, increases in demand due to lower interest rates are more likely to result in higher construction activity, which tempers price increases. Conversely, in markets with rigid or highly regulated supply, the same demand shock translates into a much larger rise in prices. Borio and Lowe (2002, pp. 28–29) also acknowledge that supply constraints can amplify the impact of low interest rates on asset prices, contributing to asset price bubbles and greater financial instability. Thus, the interaction between demand (influenced by interest rates) and supply is central to understanding asset price dynamics and will be demonstrated here by removing supply-side corrections to prices.

Research on markets that have supply-side constraints shows that, although the impact of interest rates on asset values can be dampened, delayed or transmitted through alternative channels (such as rents or leverage), the fundamental relationship persists. For example, Gyourko and Molloy (2015, pp. 1307–1310 and 1327–1330) discuss how supply constraints in housing can make prices more sensitive to demand shocks – including those arising from interest rate changes – but can also insulate prices from rate hikes when supply cannot expand.

Peng, Tam and Yiu (2008, pp. 117–120 and 126–128) provide evidence from Hong Kong's supply-constrained property market, showing that interest rates still significantly impact property values, though effects may be distorted by policy and supply restrictions.

Hendershott and Kane (1992, pp. 189–191 and 200–204) show that in markets with supply-side constraints, the link between rates and asset values can be distorted by institutional or appraisal practices, but the core relationship remains.

Lamont and Stein (1999, pp. 499–501 and 508–511) demonstrate that in segmented or credit-constrained housing markets, interest rate effects may be transmitted through changes in leverage and lending standards rather than direct price changes.

Whilst important in the context of interest rates and asset values, these studies do not present the whole picture. All four discuss the effect of interest rates. However, the first three of these studies come from a point of supply-side constraints on the market, and the fourth from controls on the provision of credit (which controls the demand side of the equation). So, while they all deal with regulation, they are all actually still dealing with an open market with various interventions affecting either supply or demand. That differs from this work in that here, all external constraints are missing.

Overall, empirical studies support the theory that even in closed or restricted markets, changes in interest rates affect the values of fixed assets, though the magnitude, speed and mechanisms often differ from those in open and competitive markets. This work provides the data proving that interest rates do indeed govern asset values where there are no external factors affecting the value.

So, classic interest rate theory and monetarism remain central to our understanding of macroeconomic policy and financial markets. While each provides distinct insights into the workings of the economy, modern economic thought recognises their interdependence. The evolution of these theories demonstrates the dynamic nature of economics as a discipline, one that continuously adapts to new data, challenges and real-world complexities. As economies grow more global and interconnected, the lessons of classic interest rate theory and monetarism will continue to help shape the policies and debates that determine economic prosperity.

Basically, neither can be used as an economic tool to affect interest rates, inflation or growth without taking into account the effect on the other factors not being targeted by the policy. If a policy is aimed solely at a growth target or an inflation target, then it can be used, but there will always be an impact elsewhere. Policymakers need to be aware of that impact, even if their role lies elsewhere.

Notes

1 The Economist (1986–present). "The Big Mac Index".
2 Letter from Jane Austen to Cassandra Austen, 9th February 1813.
3 The Bank of England, "A millennium of macroeconomic data for the UK". ONS Historical CPI Series.
4 The Bank of England, "A millennium of macroeconomic data for the UK"; ONS Historical CPI Series. See also J.H. Clapham's "*The Bank of England: A History*, Vol. II".
5 Janine Barchas, *Matters of Fact in Jane Austen: History, Location, and Celebrity* (2012) and Claudia L. Johnson, in *Jane Austen: Women, Politics, and the Novel* (1988).
6 The Bretton Woods system was agreed upon at Bretton Woods in 1944. Countries pegged their currencies to the US dollar (which was itself convertible to gold at $35 per ounce). The system collapsed in 1971 when the US ended dollar convertibility.
7 Keynes (1930, p. 207) asserted that "quasi-real" assets were a "third category of assets, namely, securities and other claims, which I have called quasi-real assets". Or were "bonds and shares, occupying an intermediate position between money and real capital assets, being more easily realisable than the latter but less liquid than money itself". I would define these as "financial assets" rather than "quasi-real assets" to allow a differentiation.
8 War loan stock was finally fully redeemed in 2015 (Bank of England press release "The Redemption of 3½% War Loan", 2015).
9 Gyourko's work, along with this book, is absolutely key in proving the link that had been expected between asset values and interest rates. It cannot be overemphasised how important his body of work, along with this book, is in 21st-century economic theory.
10 These are, up to now, the definitive works on the subject.

3 Defining Vertical Integration and Its Forms

The first stage of any work on vertical integration requires arriving at a workable definition of what we actually mean by the term 'vertical integration'. Many authors have provided definitions of vertical integration, but these definitions often take a narrow view of the term integration. The variations in types of vertical control – only one of which is strictly integration – are almost as important in understanding market dynamics as the act of integration itself, as the economic consequences to the firms concerned, and to society and the economy in general, can prove to be very similar, even when integration itself has not actually happened.

This chapter establishes the defining framework needed to understand how vertical integration creates and maintains the closed market conditions that form the core of this book's analysis. We must differentiate between the different types of integration which firms undertake in an economy, as this differentiation is crucial for understanding how some forms of integration contribute to market closure while others do not.

Understanding Vertical Integration

To understand vertical integration, we must first distinguish it from other forms of corporate combination (takeovers, mergers and acquisitions, usually of competitors).

Horizontal integration occurs when a firm takes over a direct competitor, increasing its own market share in the product or market in which it produces or sells. Savings in terms of management costs often occur following horizontal integration. The total original market share is (in theory) maintained by the new single merged organisation, but the merger of the two original management structures and possible integration of production facilities, sales forces and delivery networks usually result in cost savings in overhead. Sometimes there can also be an increased gross profit margin on sales due to the elimination of competition (but this is an area where competition authorities in all countries are very keen to prevent market exploitation).

DOI: 10.4324/9781003791553-3

This is in contrast to a further type of integration known as conglomeration. This has also been described as 'product extension' or 'market extension'. Here, a firm buys another firm which produces a product not used within the processes it requires to make its own product. Among the most well-known examples of this form of conglomeration are Hanson Trust and GEC during their peak years. Conglomeration often does not result in cost savings at either the managerial level or in the integration of production. Often firms acquired in a process of conglomeration remain as separately managed subsidiary companies to the main group, which merely sets financial targets for its new holding but otherwise remains aloof from its production and marketing activities (Chandler, 1977, pp. 315–344).

More recently, high-tech firms often integrate by buying smaller firms which have software which can enhance the offering of the acquiring firm. Obviously, these cases result in total integration of management and production into the acquiring firm, merely adding the products acquired to their own product offering. This is effectively a hybrid of vertical and horizontal integration. Lee (2018, pp. 19–20) discusses the "knowledge complementary effect" of the acquisition of technology firms by others. He asserts that this is effectively a replacement for in-house research and development spending, in that a firm, rather than spend its own money directly on research and development, will simply purchase another firm that has already carried it out. In the same way that Lee approaches the topic, Roper (2018, pp. 253–256 and 258–259) takes a more practical rather than theoretical approach to vertical integration.

Having established what vertical integration is not, we can now examine what it is and the various forms it takes.

Vertical Integration Itself

Williamson (1975, p. 82) starts the discussion of integration within manufacturing processes in straightforward terms, by asking, "given that the final [manufactured][1] product is to be assembled from a series of separable components, which of these will be bought, which will be made, and how will the latter be organised?"

Put simply, vertical integration occurs when a firm either takes over one of its suppliers or sets up its own operation to supply itself (effectively in competition with its former supplier). This is also known as backwards integration (back into a firm's supply chain, rather than forwards into the firm's customers).

By itself, this could be both a simple and an adequate definition of vertical integration. It can, however, lead to questions about the definition of a firm and its relationship with the organisation which supplies it. Coase (1937, pp. 1–20) discusses the definition of the firm comprehensively. The legal aspects of Coase's discussion are expanded on by Masten (1988, pp. 196–209). Coase alludes to the fact that within a firm the normal economic price mechanism of transactions is set aside. Instead, a 'controlling interest' transfers economic resources within the firm without necessarily any reference to the prevailing price in the market.

Broadly speaking, therefore, a firm can be described as an organisation where ultimate organisational control is exercised by one body. This controlling body could be an individual (such as an owner or a managing director) or a body such as a committee or a board of directors. This definition differentiates the firm as a single organisation from a collection of firms and individuals working in series to produce a final product over which there is no central control but rather a set of contractual relationships.

This differentiation between a firm and non-firm relationships is important within the general definition of vertical integration. It becomes of even greater importance when discussing quasi-vertical integration, which we examine later in this chapter.

Forwards and Backwards Integration

Williamson (1975, p. 102) discusses the principle of manufacturing firms integrating forwards into their customers. In his argument, he expects their customers to be wholesalers. This is a logical point of view, as, by definition, a manufacturer's customers could only be retailers directly if it had already integrated into some form of wholesaling, even if only through direct supply to retailers. Williamson later (1985, pp. 107–111) modified his argument by stating that over time manufacturers could integrate into their own customers (the wholesalers) and also into the wholesalers' customers (the retailers).

He accepts that this latter course of action would usually include integration into the wholesalers first (or as part of an overall transaction), unless the manufacturer undertook direct supply to the end consumer (which we shall see happening later in this book).

Chandler (1977, p. 287) asserts that "the first industrialists to integrate [forwards from mass production into mass distribution] … did so because existing [wholesale distributors] were unable to sell and distribute products in the volume in which they were produced". His basic argument is that when some form of technological innovation occurred, the distribution of the manufactured product often changed as much as the manufacturing process itself. Chandler cites many examples, but a good one to mention is the innovation of refrigeration, allowing meat that was killed in the Midwest of the United States to be kept fresh on its journey to the East Coast. Previously, the cattle had to be transported live from west to east, either by train or herded overland, which was a much more costly process.

Where new techniques were required in the distribution of products, Chandler tells us (1977, pp. 287–288), existing wholesalers were often reluctant to make the necessary changes. Manufacturers would, therefore, find it beneficial to set up their own distribution system to ensure their product was properly distributed. In this way, large corporations emerged, integrated from the point of manufacture (which was their initial activity) through to the point of sale, although the final retailing was often still left in the hands of independent retailers (at least initially).

The kinds of manufacturers who integrate forwards most quickly are often those involved in primary innovation. The cases of Alcoa (the first company to successfully smelt aluminium) and the Edison Company (developing the electric light bulb) both serve as good examples. In both cases, the company had produced what it perceived to be a useful product but had no existing market for it. Nobody had used either product before, and there was no infrastructure to support its use. In order to market the product swiftly and to capitalise on the fact that nobody else made the product, both companies had no choice but to retail it themselves directly to the ultimate user. In the case of Edison and the electric light bulb, the whole infrastructure of electrical power needed to be set up, from the production of generators to produce the electricity to the cable network to distribute the power (this work is highlighted by Tindall and Shi, pp. 507–508). In this instance, there were additional benefits in that the infrastructure created allowed for the invention, production and sale of an entirely new set of electrically powered machines, both domestic and industrial.

In cases of primary innovation it is also worth noting that backwards integration also occurs, as there are initially no producers to supply the necessary raw materials and components. Alcoa provides an excellent example of this phenomenon, which we examine in more detail in subsequent chapters.

Interestingly, as an example of a firm which wished to carry out its own distribution in the form outlined above, Williamson (1985, p. 109) cites the example of Kodak (photographic film processors) integrating forwards into retailing and eliminating wholesalers. To some extent, this was reversed in the United Kingdom, where Kodak entered an agreement in 1993 with a pharmaceutical wholesaler whereby that wholesaler handled Kodak sales to independent retail pharmacists.[2] This was effectively the vertical disintegration of that part of Kodak's business. This business has now ceased entirely, as commercial film processing has now almost entirely disappeared due to the fact that most cameras now capture digital images.

Vertical Control and Quasi Integration

Firms within an economy often try to control suppliers in a similar way to that found within vertical 'integration', but without actually committing capital to purchase the supplier. This is known as quasi-vertical integration, or vertical control. As with vertical integration itself, a firm can vertically control its customers, which is known as forwards vertical control.

Blair and Kaserman (1983, pp. 52–77) discuss the various types of "forward vertical control" undertaken. They suggest several "contractual alternatives" to "ownership integration" that are variously chosen by firms to control their customers. They suggest tying arrangements, output and sales revenue royalties and an entry fee as various alternatives.

Tying arrangements are where the controlling supplier specifies an amount of its product that will be purchased by the controlled purchaser. This is specified as a proportion of the total purchases of the customer, and there is an incentive for both parties to maximise the final sales made by the purchaser.

Output and sales revenue royalties are basically charges made by a supplier as a proportion of the sales made by the customer. These are very common in franchise-type operations, which we examine in detail later.

The fixed entry fee is a payment by a purchaser to the supplier for the right to buy the products produced by the supplier. This only works in the situation of a monopoly supplier.

These three elements of vertical control described by Blair and Kaserman are found in many forms of vertical control and are especially found (usually in some sort of combination) in the area of franchising, to be looked at later in this chapter.

These are all methods of forward vertical control from a controlling supplier to a controlled purchaser. Approaches to vertical control by customers towards their suppliers tend to be more subtle, in that they are terms written into contracts on such issues as quality, supply times and product labelling.

The difficulty that is bound to arise is the question of when a normal supplier customer contract becomes a relationship in which one has a measure of control over the other. This would logically seem to occur at the point where a contract starts to dictate to one party 'how' they are to carry out certain functions, as opposed to merely 'what' functions they perform. For example, a contract for one firm to supply 25 cars to another is obviously a simple supplier customer contract. It would remain so if it specified the colour of the cars, the date of delivery and the standard of manufacture. However, if it were specified that they should be made using a specific machine, when perhaps there are alternative machines available, then it is moving into the realms of being a 'controlling' contract. This issue of 'how to do', rather than 'what to do', becomes crucial in distinguishing control relationships from normal commercial contracts.

Perhaps the most often quoted example of vertical control in the United Kingdom is the case of Marks and Spencer PLC (mentioned by Auerbach, 1990, p. 4). The company has built a reputation for quality and was historically known for the strength of its own brand products (sold under the label 'St Michael'). For many years, Marks and Spencer sold only its own brand products in its stores, sourced from dedicated suppliers. In order to maintain quality standards, they kept tight controls on their suppliers, many of whom were never publicly identified, as they supplied exclusively for the 'St Michael' products.

There has been speculation about whether the relationship was one-sided in favour of the customer. However, suppliers remained content with the relationship because Marks and Spencer treated their supplier contracts as long-term partnerships and took a paternalistic approach to supplier development and support.

This last point appears to be fairly crucial in relationships of vertical control, and it could be said that without such long-term views of the relationship, on both sides, difficulties are likely to occur in cases of vertical control. This point is also highlighted by the case of Jaguar cars, which we examine later, as well as being absent in the case of the Fisher Body and General Motors case, also discussed later (Klein, 1988, pp. 201–208).

Franchising as a Form of Control

Dnes (1992, p. 3) defines franchising as when "one party, the franchisor, allows another, the franchisee, to use his trade name in operating a satellite business in return for fees". This is a useful definition, which needs no expansion, and which is therefore accepted as the definition of franchising for the purpose of this work.

Franchising is a very special form of forwards vertical control, which incorporates the elements of vertical control described above but which also has the element of what Dnes calls a "satellite business". This describes the unusual feature of the franchise, not found in other forms of vertical control, which is that the franchisee would usually not exist without the trading name and business format of the franchisor existing previously.

The best known example of a franchise operation is the McDonald's chain of restaurants, which consists of a network of independent franchisees operating under a common brand and business system. The point of the franchisee not existing without the previously established trading name of the franchisor is made by trying to imagine so many independent hamburger outlets being as successful at competing in their own local marketplace if their customers did not expect to enter the familiar 'international' McDonald's environment and receive standardised products and service.

In his conclusion, Williamson (1975, p. 263) mentions franchising only in passing. He calls it a type of "quasi integrated mode of organisation which could usefully be studied". He continues that "a sensitivity to the trade off between the incentives of autonomous enterprises and the controls of integrated structures is apt to be important in this connection". Dnes concludes (1992, p. 317) that there is such a trade-off and that franchisees achieve their "next best" earnings from the relationship. He means by this that they could theoretically earn more by not being in the relationship, but that those potentially higher earnings are outweighed by other factors, primarily the reduced risk associated with operating under an established brand with proven systems and ongoing support.

A particular factor, which Dnes understates in his analysis, is the relative safety of trading under an established brand name, with national marketing and advertising supporting the brand. Franchisees often feel that this support is worth the trade-off of additional potential profit, which in the case of franchises accrues instead to the franchisor. They do, however, tend to earn more than they would under direct employment, as they are technically working for themselves and have profit incentives to maximise the performance of the franchise.

There are several advantages to be gained by the franchisor from franchising rather than directly managing retail outlets. Generally speaking, franchising circumvents the problems of direct management control and the limitation on capital associated with integration (these issues are addressed in detail in later chapters). It does this in much the same way as other forms of vertical control, although there tends to be a greater managerial commitment to a franchise operation than in other forms of vertical control. The costs of maintaining a brand, which in most businesses are covered by revenue generated, have to be covered differently in franchising, as the benefit of the brand accrues to the franchisee. It is this that justifies the additional profit accruing to the franchisor, which tends to equate to the loss to the franchisee of the best earning potential in favour of the "next best" earnings.

There are also, depending on how the franchise agreement is structured, some franchises where there is no saving of capital accruing to the franchisor. A particular case is the retail pharmacy industry, which we will look at later, which illustrates this point.

Williamson later (1985, pp. 109–110) introduces franchises more fully, using the example of motor dealerships. He describes (quoting from Porter and Livesay, 1971, p. 195) the Ford Motor Company's requirements of its dealers. The requirements that Ford laid down might be expected to lead the company to integrate forwards into its own dealer network. However, Williamson points out that the local trading patterns which were required in the motor car market (particularly in terms of trading in used cars) meant that central managerial control would have been difficult for Ford. The company therefore introduced the concept of 'franchised' dealerships.

The franchise here is a combination of the use of the trade name of the franchisor (Ford), coupled with an obligation to buy from Ford. This latter part of motor franchises is interesting, in that the supplier is a monopoly supplier for the particular branded product, although obviously not for motor vehicles in general. Merely by being a Ford dealership, the franchisee automatically ties itself to the Ford product and could not choose to buy new vehicles elsewhere than from Ford, even if he were not contractually obliged to.

Distinguishing Integration from Other Corporate Strategies

Understanding these various forms of integration and control is crucial for the analysis that follows in this book. The UK retail pharmacy market, which provides our primary case study, exhibits all these forms of vertical relationships at different times and in different circumstances. Some pharmaceutical wholesalers have engaged in pure vertical integration by purchasing retail pharmacies outright. Others have used vertical control mechanisms, including both franchise arrangements and financial control through loan guarantees. Still others have employed hybrid strategies combining elements of integration and control.

The significance of these different approaches lies not merely in their operational characteristics but in how they are affected by market closure. Pure vertical integration closes entry to a market through direct ownership and control. Franchising creates closure through brand exclusivity and operational standardisation. Financial control mechanisms create closure through dependency relationships that limit competitive behaviour.

However, it is key, in the light of the study of interest rates on the value of assets in this sector, that the integration itself, while excluding new buyers to the existing market, does not create the closure of the market to new entrants setting up new businesses in competition. That is a role which has been assumed by the ultimate major customer in the UK retail pharmacy market – the National Health Service (NHS).

In each case, the effect of integration is to reduce the competitive pressures that would otherwise drive down profit margins and asset values in existing businesses.

The closure of the market to new entrants is actually the foundation upon which the interest rate/asset value relationship operates. In competitive markets, low asset values (and therefore higher returns on capital) would attract new entrants who would compete away the higher returns (or 'excess profits'), which cannot be done in the controlled and effectively closed market of UK retail pharmacy businesses.

In markets where vertical integration and control create non-financial barriers to entry, this competitive mechanism is impaired, allowing asset values to respond directly to changes in the cost of capital, as represented by interest rates.

The following chapters explore how these theoretical concepts apply in practice within the UK retail pharmacy sector, demonstrating how control mechanisms, as well as vertical integration, combine with regulatory barriers to create the closed market conditions necessary for testing our central hypothesis about the relationship between interest rates and asset values.

Notes

1 Williamson was discussing manufacturing processes here, but the principle can be applied equally across all sectors of economic activity.
2 Source: UniChem PLC Annual Report and Accounts for 1993.

4 The Economic Drivers of Vertical Integration

Tindall and Shi (1993, p. 510) quote John D. Rockefeller as being determined "to pay nobody a profit". They cite this as his reasoning for the integration, both forwards into distribution and backwards into suppliers of all kinds, carried out by Standard Oil of Ohio. However, as Tindall and Shi also point out (1993, p. 509), there were much more sophisticated economic factors at work in his decision to integrate, which we examine in detail throughout this chapter.

Understanding why firms choose to integrate vertically is crucial to comprehending how integration contributes to the creation of closed markets. The motivations behind integration decisions determine not only which firms will integrate but also the extent to which integration creates barriers to entry that protect incumbent operators from competitive pressures. These barriers, in turn, create the market conditions where asset values respond directly to changes in interest rates rather than to competitive forces.

There are several theoretical models which give differing explanations for vertical integration. None of these models is prescriptive – they do not tell firms how they should behave – but each attempts to explain observed patterns of integration in the real economy. These models will be critically examined in turn, with particularly looking at how each contributes to our understanding of market closure and asset valuation.

The four basic causes of vertical integration we examine are natural technological interdependency, high transaction costs within the market, defensive responses to supply problems within the market and the possibility of planned integration. To these 'usual' causes, I add a fifth model – what I term the 'insurance model' of integration – which has particular relevance to understanding asset valuation in closed markets.

Technological Interdependency

Technological interdependency is perhaps the most obvious cause of vertical integration. It occurs especially in process industries where continuous processes would create enormous transaction costs if market mechanisms were

DOI: 10.4324/9781003791553-4

employed at each stage. For example, many chemical processes lead from one to another, as do processes such as steel production. It is economically efficient for these sorts of processes to be centred on one production site, and for this reason vertical integration occurred in these industries in the early stages of technological development.

Chandler (1990, pp. 18–20) points out that in 1973 almost 95% of the largest businesses in the world fell into a very small range of manufacturing processes, primarily those involved in continuous process activities such as chemicals and petroleum. These 'mega' businesses were made up almost exclusively of firms that had integrated vertically (although many of them had also integrated horizontally). Chandler argues that continuous process industries such as these benefit significantly from large integrated investments in plant, reducing both the marginal and average cost of production. Since then we have seen more of the world's largest firms emerge within the high technology sector. However, as Lee (2018, pp. 161–164 and 167–169) demonstrates, these high-tech firms often undertake vertical integration themselves, particularly through the acquisition of complementary technologies.

Therefore, integration in manufacturing and processing industries occurs because the technological interdependency of the process makes the firm more competitive and allows it to grow at the expense of its non-integrated competitors. This technological advantage can create significant barriers to entry, as potential competitors must either develop equivalent integrated capabilities or accept higher costs from using market mechanisms across technologically interdependent processes. To develop their own integrated facilities would involve huge capital costs. Obviously, for the first movers, there was also this capital cost, but with first movers, there was the advantage of 100% or 50% market share. By the time late entrants are contemplating entering the market through capital investment, the return is lower as the potential market share is split between many more firms.

The other aspect of technological interdependency, which leads into our next discussion on transaction costs, involves the case of a supplier needing to put in place specific plant and machinery to service a particular manufacturing customer. This has been termed asset specificity. Williamson (1985, pp. 89–90) looks at this, following on from his discussion of integration occurring due to continuous (or near-continuous) technological processes. Other authors (especially both Joskow, 1988, pp. 97–102 and 105–108) and Klein, 1988, pp. 202–204) classify this as a transaction cost, and therefore further discussion of this point appears in the following section.

Chandler mentions an important factor on the issue of quality control, which is pertinent to most of the reasons for backwards integration discussed in this chapter. He says (1990, p. 482), in relation specifically to pharmaceutical manufacturers, "... the need for greater purity and more careful quality control meant that they could not risk using the same intermediaries ... Therefore, the pharmaceutical companies were less reluctant ... to build plants abroad". This observation has historical significance, though it should be noted that many generic drugs are now manufactured by third-party firms in countries such as India, representing a partial reversal of this integration trend.

Hart (1989, pp. 147–150) sets out in detail the complex theoretical arguments surrounding the issues of rewarding quality in ways which avoid the need to integrate backwards into a firm's suppliers. This issue of quality control is often a vital one in many industries and is very often tied in with an element of vertical control, if not full integration. This point is illustrated by the case of Jaguar Cars, which we examine later in this chapter.

Transaction Costs and Market Failure

Blair and Kaserman (1983, pp. 13–15) outline an argument in favour of vertical integration in terms of the reduction in transaction costs which it can theoretically achieve. The argument proceeds along the lines that where transaction costs in the marketplace are relatively low compared to the managerial costs of vertically integrating, then integration will not be profitable and therefore will not occur. Conversely, where transaction costs are high relative to the costs of internal management, integration becomes economically attractive.

There are several types of transaction costs associated with using the market when examining the economic position of both suppliers and buyers. These include items as diverse as contract monitoring costs, additional costs of liaison between suppliers and customers on technical issues, and the costs involved in initial negotiation (these costs are borne by both parties), as well as such things as advertising costs (borne primarily by the supplier). These are costs which are over and above the normal liaison costs which would occur between interdivisional managers in an integrated concern and the supervision costs of senior executives within such an entity.

Blair and Kaserman's work followed that of Williamson (1971, p. 112), who felt that vertical integration is a direct result of this type of market failure. He called the resulting integration "internalisation" – the replacement of market mechanisms with internal management systems.

Anderton (1991, p. 194) states that "productive efficiency will increase if average costs of production after the merger fall because of economies of scale". The implication here is that entrepreneurs will allow vertical integration to take place within their own firm when the cost of using the market to provide goods and services is higher than the cost of providing those same goods and services in house. This in-house provision can be achieved either by buying a supplier firm or by setting up an internal organisation to provide the supplies which a third party has previously provided.

Arrow defines market failure as "the particular case where transaction costs are so high that the existence of the market is no longer worthwhile" (1969, p. 60). From this perspective it is relatively straightforward to argue a case for vertical integration taking place as a result of market failure. Indeed, the argument could be pursued in the following vein.

There may be specific reasons (as outlined elsewhere in this chapter) for integration to take place, which may allow that integration to take place despite some net cost to the integrator. However, where such specific reasons do not exist, integrators are unlikely to integrate when the net cost to them is likely to be higher than using the market. In other words, where specific other reasons for integration do not exist, integration may often take place as a cost-saving measure. If it is cheaper to integrate than to use the market, then use of the market for that particular firm is no longer worthwhile, as transaction costs exceed the costs associated with integration. Therefore, using Arrow's definition, on an individual firm basis, integration often takes place as a result of defined market failure.

Asset Specificity and Hold-Up Problems

Joskow (1988, pp. 124–130) introduces asset specificity as another form of transaction cost which could lead to market failure. Asset specificity occurs where, in order to fulfil a contract, a supplier must make significant investments in plant and machinery which will only be useful to the supplier in fulfilling that particular contract. Suppliers needing to make such investments worry that they might lose the contract after a short period for some reason or that they could be 'held up'[1] by the purchaser seeking to renegotiate terms once the specific investments have been made. They will, therefore, seek protection from this, written into the initial contract. This protection will take account of various possible (and foreseeable) changes that may occur in the market.

The problem then arises that protection for the supplier introduces the possibility of non-compliance by the supplier, thus potentially 'holding up' the purchaser, who will similarly want protection written into the initial contract. Contracts therefore tend to become increasingly complicated. Even so, unforeseen circumstances may still occur, allowing a 'hold up' of one party by the other.

This represents a transaction cost, and it creates Joskow's potential market failure. As before, a possible solution to the market failure would be for either party to integrate (either forwards or backwards) in order to control the situation and remove this transaction cost altogether.

Asset specificity as a transactional cost is discussed by Klein (1988, pp. 213–217) in the case of Fisher Body and General Motors. This is a case of quasi-vertical integration, where General Motors had a long-term contract with Fisher Body for the supply of car bodies. Fisher invested in specific machinery for the contract, which obviously required a large capital investment. At the time the contract was written (in 1919), the balance of advantage lay with General Motors, as Fisher's largest customer. However, with the growth of the car market, Fisher chose to make it more difficult and expensive for General Motors to buy its bodies (which General Motors was contractually obliged to do). Fisher adopted the practice of locating its facilities away from General Motors' plants, increasing Fisher's costs. This led to increased profit for Fisher (and higher costs for General Motors) as Fisher's profit was calculated under what was a 'cost-plus' contract. Although the costs were Fisher's, General Motors had to both meet those costs and add on a margin for Fisher's profit, so this effectively represented Joskow's 'hold up' in action.

This case illustrates how asset specificity initially worked against the supplier in the early stages, but other transactional costs appeared later on and worked against the customer, so the balance of power often changes during the contract period. It also illustrates the point made earlier about the importance of a strong relationship in cases of vertical control.

It can be argued that market failure is a negative reason for vertical integration. While it may be accurate to characterise it this way, especially when comparing this theory to the other reasons for vertical integration examined in this chapter, it is without doubt a key factor in many real-life business decisions to integrate.

A Defensive Response to Market Conditions

Chandler (1990, p. 37) states that the motive for vertical integration by firms is "usually defensive". He argues that firms undertake vertical integration in order either to assure a steady supply of raw materials or to withhold supplies of those materials from competitors. It could be argued that the latter motivation is 'aggressive' rather than 'defensive', though the distinction may be more semantic than substantive. While the broad thrust of this argument is correct, I would temper his 'usually defensive' approach to 'often defensive'.

Chandler (1990, p. 38) adds further reasons for vertical integration in terms of the reduction of "supplier risk". These include certainty of delivery and cost control. In terms of certainty of delivery, he appears to be discussing the concept of 'just-in-time' delivery schedules, rather than the more traditional 'just-in-case' schedules. Just-in-time supply contracts are innovations which involve close working relationships between customer and supplier. As such, they can fall into the category of vertical control of suppliers by their customers, rather than full integration. The rationale for these contracts is that traditional supply methods always involved the customer in holding higher levels of stock, with the consequent higher cost to the firm of its working capital, losses through dilapidation and the increased costs of storage and insurance.

Just-in-case and just-in-time stock delivery schedules represent different inventory management philosophies. With just-in-case management, deliveries from suppliers might be set at fortnightly intervals. Inventory managers would then calculate the amount of product used or sold in an average two-week period, add one week's stock to allow for order processing and then add a margin for error of, say, 15% to prevent out-of-stock positions. The result was that a firm would hold up to four weeks' stock at any given time. Just-in-time supply chains involve the customer receiving smaller amounts of new stock in theory just as the last piece of old stock is being used or sold. Of course, this involves more risk of out-of-stock positions for the customer due to potential delays in deliveries, which would result in reduced sales. It can be a fine balance, ensuring a minimal stockholding position with no loss of sales.

Green and Sutcliffe (1987, p. 107) discuss the process of vertical integration within capitalism. They also view it as being the response of firms to uncertainties in their supply lines. They then take the view that these uncertainties lead firms either to take over their supplier firms or to set up their own internal supplier organisation to supply themselves.

Chandler's view of defensive integration is borne out by the example of Alcoa, which we examine in detail in subsequent chapters. The major example of Alcoa's integration strategy was integrating its source of bauxite for the production of aluminium, which is cited by Smith (1988, pp. 97–98). Smith tells us (p. 97) that "anxious to secure better control over his sources of supply, [Alfred] Hunt [Alcoa's president] purchased … a substantial acreage of bauxite reserves". In 1909, Smith tells us (p. 97), Alcoa was "a net seller, rather than purchaser, of bauxite". Alcoa integrated backwards into many of its supplies, including, as importantly as bauxite, power supplies.

Smith tells us (p. 27) that "the availability of electrical power was to become the main determinant of the location of production facilities [for Alcoa]". Aluminium production requires large amounts of electric power, and therefore reductions in the cost of this power feed through into a reduced average cost per unit of production. Smith states (p. 96) that "the high cost of power made it only a matter of time before the company sought to free itself … from dependence on outside sources of supply". This it achieved by a combination of purchasing hydroelectricity producers and building its own hydroelectric dams.

However, integration into its supplies of power was defensive for Alcoa, not just in terms of reducing its cost and securing its supplies of power. It is also a good example of the argument that Chandler's 'defence' against the market is often actually aggressive in its competitive effects. This argument is supported by Smith (1988, p. 96), who quotes the minutes of an Alcoa company board meeting in 1896 where it was stated that the company would have to establish or acquire hydroelectric plants in Canada, where power was relatively cheap, "to preclude the establishment in the future of works to manufacture aluminium at some of the Canadian waterpowers". This demonstrates that in the commercial world 'defensive' integration can actually be aggressive by imposing restrictions on (or barriers to) the entry of competitors, making their supply of material (or in this case, power) much more difficult and costly than it would be if the market for raw materials and supplies were free from the ownership of just one manufacturer.

This 'aggressive' aspect of defensive integration was also behind Rockefeller's first move into integration at Standard Oil (Tindall and Shi, 1993, p. 509). By integrating forwards into marketing petroleum through retail outlets, Standard Oil was able to obtain better freight rates from railroads, making its oil cheaper and more competitive than its competitors' products.

Both these examples of firms in new industries integrating support Stigler's view (1968, pp. 129–141, quoted in Williamson, 1975, p. 16). Stigler suggests that vertical integration goes through a life cycle in industries. In 'young' industries, integration is extensive. Later, disintegration occurs with further growth in the industry. This is followed by reintegration as the industry starts to decline.

Chandler (1990, p. 38) further points out that "the more concentrated the facilities of production and the more concentrated the sources of supply, then the more likely vertical integration is to occur". This can be taken as a manufacturer's reaction against a monopoly supplier, where to protect itself it may try to set up its own supply of either raw materials or components. This point is developed more fully in the section on the insurance model.

Defensive vertical integration sometimes takes place on a scale that is small compared to the total supply of a particular good or service to the integrating firm. This is said by those carrying it out both to allow them an insight into the difficulties and costs faced by suppliers in the market and to protect the buyer in instances where non-standard products or services are required.

An example of where this kind of defensive integration existed can be found in the public sector. Berkshire County Council (which was abolished in 1997 and its functions transferred to six district authorities) used to maintain a capacity in its own homes for elderly people of about 20% of its total requirement.[2] The remaining 80% was purchased from various homes within the private sector. The Council maintained its own capacity for managerial reasons so that it could negotiate with its private sector suppliers based on its own practical experience of managing homes. However, it also had a defensive economic reason for keeping its own capacity in that there were often emergency admissions into homes, which frequently took place outside normal hours. The Council could place such admissions into its own homes to avoid additional costs being charged by private-sector suppliers for 'non-standard' admission procedures in such circumstances.

Most of this discussion has centred so far on backwards integration. However, forward integration can also be carried out as a defensive response to market conditions (see the Standard Oil example above). In highly competitive industries, a reliable way of ensuring that customers remain with a firm is to purchase or control them in some way. There are many instances where this kind of defensive integration takes place, one of which is within pharmaceutical wholesaling, which we examine as a practical example in subsequent chapters.

Integration as Strategic Planning

Auerbach (1990, p. 3) argues from the perspective that any firm, of any size, has a degree of vertical integration within itself, however minimal that may be. This is entirely justifiable, as a firm, in the process of adding value to the product it will finally sell, has to integrate at least three stages. These are the purchase of its 'inputs' (perhaps raw materials or completed goods), the stage of adding value to its purchases (this is easy to see in a manufacturing concern, but in wholesaling or retailing this consists of storage, display or perhaps repackaging), and the sale of its 'outputs'.

Auerbach (1990, pp. 6–7) goes on to discuss the planning process needed in the development of new products, which, he argues, requires a high degree of vertical integration to occur successfully. This is mentioned briefly above, in the context of Alcoa and the Edison Company both needing to integrate forwards to establish new marketing structures for products that had not previously existed. Auerbach does not go into detail about the fact that both of these companies also needed to integrate backwards to create the infrastructure needed for their new products. Both of these actions would fall into the category of 'an act of planning', as the integration was planned as part of the development of both the new product and its market.

Auerbach describes (1990, p. 6) the way in which integrating in a planned manner has created advantages for many kinds of producers. He cites the planned way in which steel production in the post-war era became a global competitive free market, rather than the previous collection of national oligopolies. He contends that this could only occur through integration in a planned manner and that, therefore, planning has to be recognised as a reason for vertical integration.

A question which could be posed is whether a retailer develops a new product because of that retailer's knowledge of what its customers want or whether a product is invented for which retailers subsequently find a market. The answer to this often lies in the realm of primary innovation. Large multinational companies, especially in sectors such as electronics and pharmaceuticals, tend to have integrated research departments, which divide activities between 'pure' and 'applied' research.

The area of 'pure' research involves studying phenomena that appear interesting to see where the research might lead. This is a very expensive activity, which often produces totally wasted effort and which many companies try to avoid. However, sometimes such research can produce totally unexpected results, which prove to be extremely valuable and which can become commercial successes where an integrated firm is in a position to develop a market for the discovery. A firm which is integrated across retailing, manufacturing and original research is in a much stronger position to develop unexpected discoveries in such a way that a ready market for the finished product can be developed.

A Potential Insurance Model of Vertical Integration

Williamson (1975, p. 88) briefly mentions integration as a means of insurance but does not develop the argument as fully as its importance appears to merit. Likewise, Chandler (1990, p. 38) makes the point that if an investment is made which integrates facilities but does not reduce transaction costs, then that investment could be seen merely as a 'portfolio investment'.

Chandler (1990, p. 38) uses this point to discuss "risk". In terms of alleviating risk, it is normal to carry some form of "insurance". In this section we examine not an insurance policy per se but an alternative 'insurance'-type model of investment that has particular relevance to the understanding of asset valuations in closed markets.

In developing the 'insurance model' argument below, we should bear in mind that a firm could make any portfolio investment, for which it would achieve a return on its capital. The model developed here is of considerable interest for understanding asset valuation, despite being quite limited in its potential applications, due to factors which we also examine.

The model follows on from Chandler's point (1990, p. 38), discussed above, that the likelihood of backwards integration increases when there is only a limited number of suppliers in the market. It references the fact that supplier risk is much higher when a firm has only one supplier than when it has many suppliers.

The same principle applies when considering a firm's customers. If there is a limited market for a firm's products, then the firm will consider itself more at risk should competitors take some customers away from it, as it would be more difficult to replace them from the limited number of customers still available in the marketplace. Thus, the likelihood of forward integration increases with a limited number of customers in the marketplace. A practical example of this is found later in our examination of forward integration from the pharmaceutical wholesale sector into pharmacy retailing.

These points are important when examining the insurance motive for vertical integration (both backwards and forwards) in terms of reducing either supplier risk or the competitive risk of losing customers. This represents a relatively specific consideration, which could, in fact, be viewed as vital. It concerns the return on capital invested in vertically integrating, whether by acquisition or by investing directly in new facilities. Where such an investment is made as a defensive measure, the firm needs to be aware of the return it could make by investing the capital elsewhere. The question which, therefore, arises is whether the firm making the investment is foregoing a part of the return it could otherwise make to protect its supplies (either the cost or actual supply of them) or its customer base. Effectively, this is an insurance cost.

If it is true that part of the return on capital is foregone, then what is the 'insurance premium' that such firms are effectively paying?

This could be calculated using a relatively straightforward formula, providing all elements were known or could reasonably be estimated. The formula would be:

$$IP = RCp - RCa + MC - TC$$

where:

IP = the 'insurance premium' effectively paid
RCp = the potential return on capital invested
RCa = the actual return on capital invested
MC = the increase in management costs associated with integrating
TC = the transaction costs of using the market which are saved by integrating

Williamson (1975, p. 14) discusses the insurance premium that risk-averse individuals (and firms) are prepared to pay in order to remove risk to them. This type of insurance usually covers risk to physical assets but can equally be applied to financial risk. His discussion is not wholly relevant here, as he is discussing insurance policies, whereas we effectively have a case of self-insurance. In our case, the firm considering integration is aware of its own risks and the costs arising if the risks materialise. However, Williamson does give a useful formula for the maximum premium that will be paid for insurance, which is:

$$IP = (p + e)D$$

where p is the probability of an event occurring, and D is the damage that would impact upon the firm should that event occur. The variable e is defined by Williamson as "p for the highest risk among a particular group to be insured less p for the lowest risk among the same particular group to be insured". It is effectively the spread, within the group to be insured, of the risk of the event occurring. Therefore, e is zero for a single insured risk, as the highest risk must, by definition, precisely equal the lowest risk. This therefore gives a maximum premium that a single firm is willing to pay, stated as:

$$IP = pD$$

Here, pD is actually the financial risk that the firm believes it will incur by not integrating.

Combining these two formulae (the premium a firm is willing to pay for certainty with the cost to the firm of vertically integrating), we arrive at:

$$RCp - RCa + MC - TC = pD$$

Since pD is the maximum that the firm will pay for insurance against perceived supplier or customer risk, then the equation becomes the inequality:

$$RCp - RCa + MC - TC < pD$$

The general implication of this inequality is that when it holds true (i.e., when the additional cost of vertically integrating is less than the perceived risk of not integrating), then vertical integration is likely to take place.

However, the inequality is not complete, as there are additional downside risks of integrating into either a firm's suppliers or its customers, which must be considered.

On the supply side (i.e., where the integrator is the buyer of supplies from a supplier who becomes the target for integration), the formula is only completely relevant in a situation where tight markets exist within an economy (i.e., where production is close to capacity). Where the market is tight, the formula holds good, as the supplier would have other opportunities to sell its products. Other suppliers would probably also be working close to or even at capacity and could therefore charge a premium to new potential customers, as they would have to switch supply away from their existing customers, assuming they were even able to supply the additional volume required. This could lead to the situation where supplies are difficult or costly to obtain, increasing the integrator firm's average cost of production and reducing its competitiveness.

However, in a slack market, suppliers may tend to reduce their selling prices in order to maintain production and keep their average cost of production as low as possible so that they can maintain profitability. They will also be actively seeking new customers to take up the slack in their production capacity.

In slack market conditions, therefore, the probability (p) of losing supplies, or of the supplier increasing prices by an unwarranted amount, is significantly reduced. The potential damage (D) caused by this could remain the same or probably even decrease. The greater the number of potential suppliers in the market, the more the potential damage caused by any individual supplier will reduce. The cumulative effect of these changes means that in a slack market pD will reduce, perhaps significantly. Since the other side of the inequality, RCp – RCa + MC – TC will remain broadly similar under such conditions, then RCp – RCa + MC – TC is less likely to be smaller than the reduced pD.

We can deduce from this that, where the potential integrator is a customer contemplating integrating backwards into a supplier, integration is less likely to occur in conditions of slack markets than it is within tight markets. By reversing the above arguments, it can easily be deduced that the converse is true and that a supplier is more likely to integrate forwards into its customers in periods of slack market conditions.

Practical Application of the Insurance Model

This discussion of the potential problem of market conditions changing after integration has some connection to the discussion above on just-in-case and just-in-time stockholding methods. These in turn are partly derived from Chandler's discussion of supplier risk (Chandler, 1990, p. 38). If integration had not taken place within the tight market, then the firm might be able to pass on some of its costs to its suppliers by stipulating tight delivery schedules to keep down its stockholdings.

The problems associated with changing market conditions and integration, highlighted here, are not, however, encountered only in the case of full integration. They may also occur when other forms of vertical control are undertaken. In trying to pass on problems associated with stockholding in a slack market, the controlling firm may find itself bound by contracts entered into during tighter trading conditions. This relates again to the arguments put forwards by Joskow (1988, pp. 117–133) on asset specificity. These have been discussed above, and the additional point to be made here is that long-term contracts, even without the need for investment in specific assets, may allow a hold-up of one or the other of the parties when market conditions change in a way that could not have been foreseen when the contract was written.

The insurance model theory can be illustrated by a hypothetical, but plausible, example.

Let us suppose that Widgets Ltd, a manufacturer, buys vital components from supplier Bloggs Ltd. If Bloggs is one of a number of potential suppliers in the market which could supply virtually identical products at virtually the same total cost to Widgets (i.e., price to Widgets plus any transport costs), then the damage (D) in financial terms to Widgets of Bloggs ceasing supply for any reason would be very low or possibly even zero. Since the probability (p) of any event occurring is always between zero and one, then pD will also be either very small or actually zero, so it is unlikely that RCp – RCa + MC – TC will be less than pD, and integration will not occur.

However, if Bloggs is a monopoly supplier, then the financial cost to Widgets of Bloggs' failure to supply would be much greater. Widgets would need to assess this in some way, but let us suppose that it estimates the net costs likely to be incurred by Widgets as a result of such a failure to be £1 million per annum. We can see that this assessment of greater risk from a monopoly supplier follows from Chandler's principle of vertical integration occurring more often where sources of supply are concentrated.

If Widgets further assesses the probability that Bloggs will cease supply at 50%, then pD can be calculated at £500,000 (0.5 × £1,000,000). This then becomes the maximum 'premium' that Widgets would be prepared to pay to remove that risk of Bloggs ceasing supply.

Looking at the other side of the equation, let us assume that Widgets has sufficient capital available to invest in some form of supply assurance. We can imagine that there are three ways in which it could invest that capital: purchasing Bloggs Ltd, setting up its own internal organisation to replace supplies coming from Bloggs, or investing in an area of its own manufacturing field entirely unrelated to its supplies from Bloggs Ltd. Let us assume that each of the three investments would cost £10,000,000. If the two versions of vertical integration were to yield an annual return of 8% and the internal investment a return of 12%, then the potential return had that capital been invested elsewhere rather than in integrating (RCp) will be £1,200,000 per annum and the actual return on capital invested in either form of integration (RCa) will be £800,000. Let us assume here that the increase in management costs associated with integrating (MC) and the transaction costs of using the market which are saved by integrating (TC) are equal at £10,000 each. The calculation (RCp – RCa + MC – TC) will be:

$$£1,200,000 - £800,000 + £10,000 - £10,000 = £400,000.$$

This £400,000 represents the amount of profit foregone by the investing firm (Widgets Ltd) through vertically integrating. Since this £400,000 is less than the £500,000 that the firm would be willing to pay for insurance to assure its supplies, we would predict, using the 'insurance model', that vertical integration will take place in this case.

If we extend this argument one stage further, we could find that this insurance model affects the price paid for, and therefore the value of, companies that are bought in order to be integrated (whether forwards or backwards). This has particular relevance to understanding asset valuation in closed markets, which we examine in detail in later chapters.

Integration and Market Closure

Understanding these various drivers of vertical integration is crucial to comprehending how integration contributes to the creation of closed markets. Each of the motivations examined – technological interdependency, transaction cost reduction, defensive strategies, planned integration and risk insurance– can contribute to market closure, but they do so through different mechanisms and to different degrees.

Technological interdependency creates market closure through the requirement for substantial capital investment and technical expertise to achieve competitive efficiency. Transaction cost considerations create closure by making integrated structures more efficient than market alternatives, raising the barriers for non-integrated competitors. Defensive integration creates closure by controlling key inputs or customer relationships, making it difficult for new entrants to establish viable businesses. Planned integration creates closure by allowing integrated firms to coordinate activities across the value chain in ways that independent operators cannot match. The insurance model creates closure by allowing integrated firms to accept lower returns on individual activities because they reduce overall business risk.

In each case, the effect is to create barriers to entry that protect incumbent firms from competitive pressures. In perfectly competitive markets, such protection would be eroded by new entrants attracted by above-normal returns. However, where integration creates substantial barriers to entry, this competitive mechanism is impaired.

This impairment of competitive forces creates the conditions where asset values can respond directly to changes in the cost of capital, as represented by interest rates, rather than being driven primarily by competitive pressures. This is the foundation of the relationship between interest rates and asset values that forms the central hypothesis of this book.

We will go on to look at how these theoretical principles apply in practice, using the UK retail pharmacy sector as a detailed case study of how vertical integration and regulatory barriers, working either together or separately, create the conditions of a closed market. Either will then create the ideal model for proving the interest rate theory.

Notes

1 'Hold-ups' and 'holding up' are used here in the sense of forcing somebody to do what they would not normally wish to do, usually involving extracting money or concessions.

2 Source: Berkshire County Council Social Services Department briefing to members of Bracknell Forest Borough Council, 3rd October 1994, committee papers.

5 Effects and Limitations of Vertical Integration

Having examined the drivers of vertical integration in the previous chapter, we now turn to an equally important question, which is 'what are the consequences of integration, both for the firms undertaking it and for the broader economy?' Understanding these effects is crucial to our analysis of how integration contributes to market closure and, ultimately, to the relationship between interest rates and asset values that forms the central thesis of this book.

The effects of vertical integration are complex and multifaceted, encompassing both benefits and drawbacks for integrating firms and both positive and negative consequences for economic efficiency and competition. This chapter is not intended as a comprehensive review of the monopolistic effects of integration on an economy as a whole, which would require a separate volume. Rather, it provides a focused examination of the effects as they relate to individual firms and to the creation of closed market conditions.

The analysis reveals a fundamental tension. While vertical integration can generate significant efficiencies and innovations that benefit both consumers and the economy as a whole, it can also create barriers to competition that allow incumbent firms to maintain above-normal profits, thereby increasing prices to customers. It is this latter effect that creates the conditions where asset values respond primarily to changes in the cost of capital rather than to competitive pressures.

Competitive Implications

The competitive effects of vertical integration have long been a subject of debate among economists and policymakers. The debate centres on whether integration primarily enhances efficiency (thereby benefiting consumers through lower costs and improved products) or creates anti-competitive effects (thereby harming consumers through reduced competition and higher prices).

Smith (1988, pp. 276–277) discusses the American oligopoly in the production of aluminium in the early post-war years. He points out the benefits of long-term price stability to producers in a capital-intensive sector of

DOI: 10.4324/9781003791553-5

production like aluminium. There tends to be greater long-term price stability in an oligopoly, where a few producers realise that their long-term interests may not be served by intensive price competition.

Smith (1988, p. 277) goes on to state that "[the industry] was more likely to enjoy a higher degree of price discipline than one with a large number of small producers, but the mere desire for price stability was not enough to produce it. The crucial enabling factor was the control of supplies that could be regulated to demand". This last observation is important in understanding the potential anti-competitive effects of vertical integration, as the control of supplies mentioned here resulted from the vertical integration undertaken by Alcoa (discussed in detail in the previous chapter).

However, as Smith points out in his discussion, price stability is not only a benefit to producers but also to customers for those raw materials. While there is significant and interesting debate about the extent to which an economy suffers from higher but stable prices, as opposed to lower but unstable prices, it is beyond the scope of this work to resolve that question.

The key point for our analysis is that if integration leads to a monopoly or an oligopoly, then higher prices to customers may result. This is likely to be detrimental to overall economic welfare, although there may be circumstances where there are offsetting benefits. Where integration does not lead to a monopoly or an oligopoly, then the overall effect on an economy is likely to be beneficial, as production is likely to become more efficient.

The Role of Barriers to Entry

The competitive implications of vertical integration depend crucially on whether integration creates significant barriers to entry for potential competitors. Where integration occurs primarily for efficiency reasons, such as technological interdependency or transaction cost reduction, and where potential competitors can achieve similar integration, then the competitive effects are likely to be benign or even positive.

However, where integration is used defensively to control scarce inputs or customer relationships, or where the scale of integration creates barriers that are difficult for new entrants to overcome, the competitive effects become more problematic. In such cases, integration can lead to market closure that protects incumbent firms from competitive pressures.

This protection from competition is what creates the conditions for the interest rate to asset value relationship that forms the core of our analysis. As looked at above, in competitive markets, above-normal profits attract new entrants who, through competition, reduce excess returns. Therefore, they keep asset values tied to their fundamental earning power rather than to the cost of capital. In markets where integration or regulation has created barriers to entry, this competitive mechanism is impaired, leading asset values to respond more directly to changes in interest rates.

Research and Development Benefits

One of the most significant positive effects of vertical integration is its impact on research and development activities. This effect is particularly important in knowledge-intensive industries but has broader applications across many sectors of the economy.

Applied research examines existing discoveries (made through pure research) and looks at how these discoveries could be applied to market opportunities. An integrated firm has a significant advantage in this field, as the research department can communicate with the marketing and sales functions at an early stage to ensure that what is being developed is a marketable commodity. The failure of many new products can often be attributed to insufficient liaison between research and commercial functions. The Sinclair C5 electric vehicle serves as an example of the failure of a new product, where the design concept was technically interesting, but insufficient liaison had taken place to determine whether there was a potential market for the product in its proposed form.

'Applied' research also covers the area where an integrated retailer asks its research department whether a particular product could be developed from existing technology, because market research indicates that there is demand for such a product. The personal computer represents an interesting example of this, where a whole new supply industry was established by diverting an existing industrial-scale technology into a different market.

Vertical integration can also facilitate what economists call 'knowledge spillovers' between different stages of the value chain. When firms are integrated, innovations at one stage can more easily be communicated to and exploited at other stages. This can lead to cumulative innovative effects that would be more difficult to achieve in a market relationship between suppliers and customers, where firms have incentives to protect their own innovations from competitors, even those in adjacent stages of the value chain.

It is important to note that this reason for, or result from, vertical integration is generally positive from a broader economic perspective, as opposed to some other motivations for integration, which can be viewed as having negative effects on overall economic efficiency. The research and development benefits of integration contribute to technological progress and innovation, which ultimately benefits consumers and the whole economy.

Capital Requirements and Management Costs

There are significant drawbacks to integrating vertically, either forwards or backwards. If there were not, we would tend to find that every industry would become fully integrated. The existence of non-integrated firms across most sectors of the economy suggests that integration involves substantial costs and limitations.

Blair and Kaserman (1983, p. 79) briefly mention the two main issues associated with full integration, namely those of capital cost and managerial problems. These issues merit detailed examination, as they often represent the primary constraints on integration strategies.

Capital Investment and Financial Risk

The first problem relates to the cost of integrating. The primary issue here is the amount of capital required to integrate, either by purchasing existing facilities or by setting up new ones. When examining industrial processes, the cost of setting up a manufacturing plant can be enormous. There may be less financial risk if the cost of these facilities can be passed 'upstream' to a supplier. Of course, the supplier will then attempt to pass some of the risk back to the customer, as described in our discussion of asset specificity in the previous chapter.

However, as great as the risk involved in investing capital in vertically integrated assets may be, the real difficulty that can be encountered is in actually raising the capital needed to make the investment, if that is what a firm wishes to do. Banks and financial institutions examine very carefully the leverage of firms that they are supporting.

As an example, if a firm has capital employed of £30,000 and outstanding borrowing of £12,000, then its leverage is 40%. This means that 40% of its capital is provided by lenders and 60% by its owners. If the firm then purchases its supplier, costing £40,000, its capital employed will rise to £70,000 (assuming the actual value of assets that it acquires is £40,000). If the proprietors contribute no additional capital to fund the purchase, then borrowing would rise to £52,000, and leverage would increase to 74%.

Banks and other lenders generally prefer not to see the leverage of a company rise above 50%, as higher leverage increases their risk of losses. Therefore, in the example above, the firm would find it difficult to raise the capital necessary to integrate into its supplier without either contributing additional equity capital or accepting higher borrowing costs to compensate lenders for the increased risk.

This capital constraint can be particularly binding for smaller firms, creating a competitive advantage for larger firms that have better access to capital markets. This dynamic can contribute to market concentration and, potentially, to the creation of barriers to entry that protect integrated incumbents from smaller potential competitors.

Managerial Complexity and Control

There is also a significant managerial cost involved in integrating, both vertically and especially horizontally. This cost is accounted for in the insurance model discussed in the previous chapter, when comparing the cost of using the market with the additional costs of managing 'in-house' activities.

This managerial cost takes several forms. These include costs (such as employment taxes) on direct employment, supervisory costs, the costs associated with the 'downtime' of direct employees (sick leave, training and social interaction) and the cost of providing services for employees. The latter includes both direct services, such as office accommodation (and the cost of the water cooler!), and indirect services, such as human resource management. It has often been estimated that 8% of an employee's productive time should be included in calculating managerial overhead costs.[1]

A firm can often save some of these management costs, especially in the field of professional services, by outsourcing the function concerned to consultants or specialist service providers. The term consultant is used here in its broadest sense, to include all professional firms providing services to other firms on a non-directly employed basis.

Probably the most commonly used example of this kind of outsourcing to save on managerial costs is the use of firms of solicitors. Only the largest British firms have their own legal departments (although most, at least quoted, have legally qualified staff performing the role of Company Secretary). Much legal work is outsourced to firms of solicitors, often retained by the company on a continuing basis. However, many other professional services and also manual services (e.g., office cleaning services) are often outsourced by firms in order to save the managerial cost of having the service integrated. Bracknell Forest Borough Council found it saved 8% of the cost of its office cleaning by outsourcing the service.[2]

Auerbach (1990, p. 13) expands on this point in terms of modern multinational industries, stating that "do it yourself activities become less of a necessity for multinational enterprises attempting to function at a world class level, as they may purchase financial, marketing and other infrastructures ... when it seems advantageous to do so".

While there is undeniably a cost in the management of integrated functions, this must be offset against an important benefit – that of flexibility. As mentioned in the example of Berkshire County Council's homes for elderly people in the previous chapter, there is often significant flexibility in managing one's own operations, and this is particularly valuable in terms of the cost of using the market for non-standard or emergency requirements.

This point can be emphasised by the example of payroll services, which was a traditionally integrated service in British industry. The outsourcing of payroll services was one of the greatest growth areas of both the financial services and computer services sectors during the 1980s.

However, many firms which were considering outsourcing their payroll found that the cost of using external providers was attractive only for straightforward regular payments. In a practical example from 1996, it was found that as soon as changes occurred to the payroll, the price charged by the payroll agency rose quite steeply. Analysis by the firm concerned showed that if (as was the case with this firm) there was a rapid rate of staff turnover, with bonus payments, overtime and regular changes in hours worked, it was actually cheaper to run a small in-house payroll section rather than outsource the service.[3]

The Problem of Non-Core Activities

This managerial problem associated with vertical integration is closely linked to a third possible problem of integrating, which is that of the 'non-core activity'. This problem is highlighted by the number of occasions on which large companies sell one of their divisions "in order to concentrate on core activities".

This is more usually a problem associated with horizontal integration or conglomeration, as vertical integration would tend to keep a firm focused on its own core value chain. However, there are instances in which it could be relevant to a vertical integrator. The idea is that a firm operates in a marketplace which it knows and feels comfortable with. It may, however, decide to vertically integrate some of its support functions or integrate into its customers' operations.

Having integrated backwards into support services, the firm may find that it has acquired a capability to supply other markets with those support services. Those other markets may be compatible with its own existing market, and organisational synergies could occur, which allow for more efficient exploitation of that marketplace. However, it is more likely that the markets acquired need specialised knowledge and that executives in the integrating firm spend a disproportionate amount of time managing a relatively small part of the total organisation. The firm could then decide to disintegrate, releasing the capital employed to be used within its own core business.

When a firm integrates forward into its customers, it can enter a completely different market, passing, for example, from wholesaling into retailing. This can be a difficult transition to make, and firms often conclude that vertical control is preferable so that the firm itself can concentrate on its own core business and leave the customer-facing activities to its existing customers or to specialists in that function.

The Case for Vertical Control over Full Integration

Given the significant costs and limitations of full vertical integration discussed above, it is worth examining why firms might choose vertical control mechanisms as set out above over complete integration. Auerbach (1990, p. 4) states a widely held belief that Japan achieved economic success through a system of manufacturers vertically controlling their suppliers. The reason he cites is that this allows for improved quality and inventory control. The question arising is whether Japanese firms would still have been successful had they fully integrated, rather than merely controlling, their suppliers, given the potential benefits of at least comparable control on inventory levels and quality.

Looking at some of the downside risks associated with integration itself, we can see that there are advantages in a 'halfway house' approach, providing many of the benefits of integration, but without some of the associated risks and management costs.

Capital Efficiency Benefits

The primary benefit of vertical control, including many forms of franchising, is the saving of large amounts of capital, which has been discussed above. This particular benefit is illustrated by the case of Jaguar Cars in the early 1980s. Underwood (1989, pp. 70–77) points out that Jaguar needed to control the quality of its components much more tightly in order to improve the quality of its cars, which were losing their reputation as high-quality premium models. However, as a struggling car manufacturer, needing to invest capital in its own processes, it could not and did not wish to devote capital resources to integrate backwards into its own component suppliers.

Underwood explains how Jaguar introduced its own quality thresholds within its supplier firms through a process of negotiation, as well as providing its suppliers with as much technical help and expertise as they needed to improve quality. Jaguar approached the controlling relationship as a positive long-term partnership and realised that if it was not going to take over its suppliers (which it could not do, lacking the capital required), then it would have to work more closely with them in its own long-term interests. This approach also supports the points made earlier about the importance of the strength of the relationship being important in the case of vertical control, as well as recognising the two-way benefits of the relationship.

Risk Distribution and Flexibility

Vertical control can also be used as a variant of forward integration, with similar capital efficiency benefits. This approach allows the controlling firm to influence and coordinate downstream activities without accepting the full capital commitment and management burden of ownership. In volatile markets, this flexibility can be particularly valuable, as control relationships can often be modified or terminated more easily than ownership relationships can be unwound.

The insurance benefits discussed in the previous chapter can often be achieved through control mechanisms without the full capital commitment required for integration. A firm can reduce its supplier or customer risks through contractual arrangements, franchise systems, or financial relationships that create dependency and loyalty without requiring outright ownership.

When Integration Might Fail

Understanding when and why vertical integration fails provides additional insights into the conditions that affect asset values in markets closed in this way. This failure can be either by not occurring when it might be expected or by it being reversed through disintegration.

Integration failures often occur when management complexity exceeds the benefit of integrating. Where the cost of coordinating integrated activities exceeds the benefits from avoiding market transactions, then it is likely that integration will fail.

Likewise, when the capital requirement of integrating exceeds available resources, or the cost of additional capital requirements exceeds the savings from integration, then failure is likely.

Market conditions may sometimes change. Where changes in technology, regulation or competitive conditions eliminate the original rationale for integration, then problems will occur.

Finally, where the optimal scale of operation at different stages of the value chain varies significantly, inefficiencies are likely to occur in integrated structures. This is often seen in very large-scale businesses, where call centres and websites are overwhelmed by the demand for their services.

These failure modes help explain why some markets remain competitive while others become closed through integration. Markets are more likely to remain open and competitive when integration is difficult or costly to achieve and more likely to become closed when integration provides sustainable advantages that are difficult for new entrants to replicate.

The retail pharmacy market case studies that we look at in later chapters provide examples of both successful integration and control mechanisms and instances where market changes led to disintegration. These are separate to the regulatory mechanisms that also lead to the closed market in this sector.

These examples illustrate how the balance between integration benefits and costs can shift over time and how regulatory and market changes can alter the viability of different organisational strategies.

The Effect of Integration on Asset Valuations

The effects and limitations of vertical integration examined in this chapter have direct implications for understanding asset valuation in closed markets. The key insight is that integration and control mechanisms can create sustainable competitive advantages that protect firms from the normal competitive pressures that would otherwise drive asset values towards their fundamental earning power.

Where integration creates significant barriers to entry, incumbent firms can maintain above-normal returns without attracting new competitors. In such circumstances, the primary variable affecting the value of business assets becomes the discount rate applied to expected future cash flows, which correlates directly with interest rates.

This creates the conditions where asset values respond primarily to changes in the cost of capital rather than to competitive forces. The stronger the barriers to entry to a market created by either integration or regulation, the more directly asset values will respond to interest rate changes. The weaker the barriers, the more asset values will be determined by competitive forces and fundamental business performance.

This relationship between closed markets and interest rates forms the theoretical foundation for thc cmpirical analysis presented in later chapters, where we demonstrate how changes in interest rates drive changes in asset values in the closed (mainly by regulation, but also taking account of integration factors) market created in the UK's regulated pharmacy sector.

Notes

1 Barclays Bank Clerical Work Improvement Programme 1981, internal documentation.
2 Internal report to Bracknell Forest Borough Council Finance Committee, 1992, committee papers.
3 Confidential source material.

6 Vertical Disintegration

When Firms Separate

Having examined the drivers, forms and effects of vertical integration in the preceding chapters, we now turn to what might appear to be the opposite phenomenon, which is vertical disintegration. While the literature on vertical integration is extensive, the study of disintegration has received comparatively less attention, despite its equal importance in understanding market dynamics and the evolution of industrial structure. Understanding why firms choose to reverse previously integrated operations provides crucial insights into the conditions under which integration can either create or destroy value and helps explain the dynamics of whether markets are either open or closed over time.

Vertical disintegration is the process by which previously integrated operations are separated into independent units. It represents more than simply the reverse of integration. It reflects fundamental changes in market conditions, technology, regulation or firm capabilities that alter the cost-benefit calculation that initially drove integration. The study of disintegration therefore provides a natural experiment in understanding the true drivers of integration decisions and their sustainability over time.

This chapter examines the theoretical foundations of disintegration, the empirical conditions that drive it, and its implications for market structure and competition. The analysis demonstrates that disintegration decisions follow predictable patterns related to changing transaction costs, technological developments and market evolution. Understanding these patterns is essential to our broader investigation of market closure and asset valuation, as disintegration can transform closed markets into competitive ones, fundamentally altering the relationship between interest rates and asset values.

Understanding Disintegration

The phenomenon of vertical disintegration challenges simplistic notions that integration is always preferable to market transactions. If integration were universally superior, we would expect to see a steady trend towards greater vertical integration across industries over time. Instead, we observe cycles of

DOI: 10.4324/9781003791553-6

integration and disintegration, suggesting that the optimal organisational form depends on specific circumstances that change over time.

Coase's insight that firms exist because they can sometimes organise transactions more efficiently than markets provides the theoretical foundation for understanding both integration and disintegration.[1] When the costs of organising transactions within a firm rise relative to the costs of using market mechanisms, disintegration becomes economically rational. This can occur for several reasons. These can be that markets may have become more efficient due to technological improvements or institutional developments or that internal coordination costs may have risen due to either bureaucratic growth or loss of entrepreneurial focus. Also, external conditions may have changed in ways that reduced the benefits of integration while increasing its costs.

The decision to disintegrate is therefore not an admission of failure in terms of the original integration decision but rather an appropriate response to changed circumstances. This dynamic view of organisational boundaries helps explain why we observe both integration and disintegration occurring simultaneously across different industries and even within the same industry at different times.

There is often reluctance on behalf of management to change direction, as it is perceived that this is an admission of failure. This is a wrong approach, as changing strategy to change prevailing circumstances is a positive attribute. Too many organisations have (and are encouraged by their financiers to have) a corporate strategy. This is often set in stone for a period, and followed unswervingly, despite changes in external conditions.

Williamson's transaction cost analysis provides additional insight into disintegration decisions.[2] When asset specificity decreases, uncertainty falls, or transaction frequency changes, the cost-benefit analysis of internal versus market organisation can shift decisively in favour of market transactions. Similarly, when the threat of opportunistic behaviour diminishes (perhaps due to improved contract enforcement or the development of reputation mechanisms) then the need for hierarchical control may disappear.

The overall pharmaceutical sector provides several examples of this dynamic. Technological advances in information systems have reduced the transaction costs of coordinating supply chains, making vertical disintegration feasible in areas where integration was previously necessary. Similarly, regulatory changes that increase transparency and standardisation can reduce opportunism risks, enabling market-based coordination where hierarchical control was previously required.

The Cost-Benefit Analysis of Internal Management

The core of any disintegration decision lies in comparing the costs and benefits of internal management against market alternatives. This analysis involves several dimensions that may not be immediately apparent when integration decisions are first made but become clear as market conditions evolve and managerial experience accumulates.

Internal Management Costs

The costs of internal management extend far beyond simple administrative expenses. They include the opportunity costs of managerial attention, the rigidities introduced by hierarchical decision-making, the loss of market discipline that comes with eliminating arm's length transactions and the reduced incentives for innovation that often accompany bureaucratic growth.

In the pharmaceutical wholesale sector, we observed examples of firms that discovered their integrated retail operations were consuming disproportionate management attention relative to their contribution to overall profitability. When wholesale margins came under pressure due to regulatory changes, management's focus necessarily shifted to defending the core business, making the diversionary effects of retail integration increasingly costly.[3]

The loss of market discipline represents a particularly subtle but important cost of integration. When divisions within an integrated firm transact with each other, they lack the performance benchmarks that come from competing in open markets. This can lead to complacency, cost inflation and reduced innovation. External suppliers facing competitive pressure often outperform internal divisions that operate in protected environments.[4]

Furthermore, integration can create bureaucratic layers that slow decision-making and reduce entrepreneurial responsiveness. As organisations grow through integration, they often develop internal procedures and approval processes that, while necessary for coordination, reduce the flexibility that smaller independent firms can maintain. In rapidly changing markets, this loss of agility can outweigh the coordination benefits of integration.

Through the discussions held with key players in the sector, it was noted that larger integrated firms had several layers of area management, district management and regional management. These were fixed overhead costs that smaller retail groups did not have, so that when margins were squeezed by contractual changes (outlined below), the larger retail groups struggled to meet the fixed overhead costs from their reduced retailing margins.

Market Alternative Benefits

Disintegration becomes attractive when market alternatives offer superior performance in key areas. These advantages can manifest in several ways. Specialist suppliers may achieve economies of scale unavailable to integrated divisions, competitive markets may drive innovation faster than internal development or market transactions may provide flexibility that internal operations cannot match.

The rise of specialist service providers in many industries exemplifies how market alternatives can become superior to integration. In pharmaceutical distribution, specialist technology providers emerged who could offer inventory management and ordering systems superior to those developed internally by integrated firms. These specialists achieved economies of scale by serving multiple clients and faced competitive pressure to continuously improve their offerings.[5]

Market transactions also provide flexibility benefits that internal operations often cannot match. Firms using market suppliers can more easily adjust capacity in response to demand fluctuations, switch suppliers when better alternatives emerge and access innovations developed by specialised firms. Integrated operations, by contrast, represent fixed commitments that may become liabilities when market conditions change.

The option value of market transactions deserves particular emphasis. When firms rely on market suppliers, they retain the ability to change suppliers, renegotiate terms, or bring operations in-house if circumstances warrant. Integrated operations foreclose these options, creating switching costs that may become prohibitively expensive if the initial integration decision proves suboptimal (e.g., through the closure of whole divisions).

Dynamic Considerations

The cost-benefit analysis of internal management must take account of dynamic factors that often change over time. Market conditions evolve, technologies advance and regulatory environments shift in ways that can fundamentally alter the relative advantages of integration versus market transactions.

Technological change represents perhaps the most important dynamic factor in disintegration decisions. Those same electronic data interchange (EDI) systems in wholesale distribution, for example, reduced the coordination costs that originally drove vertical integration in many supply chains. When suppliers and customers could communicate orders, delivery schedules and inventory levels in real time, the need for hierarchical coordination diminished.[6]

Similarly, improvements in contract law and enforcement mechanisms can reduce the transaction costs that initially drove integration. When courts become more sophisticated in interpreting commercial relationships and more effective in enforcing agreements, firms may find that complex supply relationships can be managed through contracts rather than hierarchy.

Regulatory changes also create dynamics that favour disintegration in some circumstances. The introduction of competition into previously monopolised markets, for example, can make vertical integration a liability rather than an asset. Firms that built integrated structures to navigate regulated environments may find these structures inappropriate for competitive markets.

Market Evolution and Changing Strategies

The evolution of market structure over time provides natural examples of the dynamics of integration and disintegration. Markets that begin as fragmented and become concentrated through integration may later fragment again as new technologies or regulatory changes alter competitive dynamics. Understanding these evolutionary patterns helps explain when disintegration becomes strategically necessary rather than merely optional.

Maturity and Standardisation Effects

As markets mature, standardisation often reduces the need for integration that had been necessary during earlier developmental phases. In emerging markets, integration may be needed to ensure quality control, coordinate complementary investments or manage technological uncertainty. Within those maturing markets, standards emerge and these coordination problems diminish, making market transactions more viable.

The pharmaceutical wholesale sector illustrates this pattern. As the UK retail pharmacy market developed, especially from the mid-1980s onwards (and especially from the mid-1990s), wholesalers often integrated forward into retail to protect their market share against newly emerging multiple chains of retail pharmacy businesses. As the market became more mature, this integration became less necessary and in some cases counterproductive.[7]

Standardisation also enables the emergence of specialist suppliers who can achieve economies of scale by serving multiple clients. In mature markets, these specialists often outperform integrated divisions that cannot achieve similar scale in specialised functions. This creates pressure for disintegration as firms recognise they can achieve better performance through market transactions than through internal operations.

Competitive Dynamics

Changes in competitive intensity can also drive disintegration. Integration strategies that made sense in concentrated markets may become liabilities as competition intensifies. Integrated structures may reduce the flexibility needed to respond to competitive threats or create cost disadvantages relative to more focused competitors.

The deregulation of many industries has created exactly this dynamic. Firms that built integrated structures to manage regulated environments often found these structures inappropriate for competitive markets. In such cases, disintegration became necessary to restore competitive fitness rather than simply being an option for improving efficiency.

Conversely, markets that become more concentrated may create new opportunities for integration as coordination becomes more manageable with fewer players. The dynamics of integration and disintegration therefore depend crucially on the evolution of market structures and competitive intensity.

Technological Disruption

Technological disruption represents perhaps the most dramatic driver of disintegration. New technologies can eliminate the coordination problems that originally drove integration, enable new forms of market organisation, or create entirely new competitive dynamics that favour different organisational forms.

The rise of Internet-based technologies provides numerous examples of technologically driven disintegration. Firms that integrated to manage information flows may find that electronic networks make external coordination just as efficient as an internal hierarchy. Similarly, technologies that reduce monitoring costs may enable market relationships that were previously too costly to manage.[8]

In some cases, technological change makes previous integration decisions obsolete by eliminating the underlying coordination problems. In other cases, new technologies create opportunities for different forms of integration that make previous approaches disadvantageous. Understanding these technological dynamics is crucial for predicting when disintegration will become strategically more attractive.

Case Studies in Disintegration

Examining specific instances of disintegration provides concrete insights into the factors that drive these decisions and their consequences for the performance of individual firms and market structure. The following cases, drawn from the pharmaceutical sector but also including examples from other industries, illustrate different types of disintegration and their underlying causes.

Case Study 1: Retail Disintegration from Wholesaling in Pharmaceutical Distribution

One of the clearest examples of systematic disintegration in the pharmaceutical sector involved several major wholesalers' decisions to exit retail operations during the late 2010s and early 2020s. These firms had integrated forward into retail during the 1990s, continuing into the early 2010s. This was driven by concerns about securing distribution outlets (keeping customers) but also about rolling retail margins into their profits.

However, several factors combined to make this integration strategy unsustainable. Regulatory changes reduced wholesale margins, making the capital and management attention devoted to retail operations increasingly costly. Simultaneously, the retail pharmacy market became more competitive as multiples expanded and independent pharmacies became more sophisticated in their purchasing and operations.[9]

The disintegration process typically involved selling retail operations to management teams, independent pharmacists or retail chains. In most cases, these sales resulted in improved performance for both the divested retail operations and the parent wholesale companies. The retail operations benefitted from focused management attention and elimination of transfer pricing complications, while wholesale operations could redirect resources to defending their core business.

This pattern illustrates several important principles of disintegration. Firstly, integration that made sense under one set of market conditions became counterproductive as those conditions changed. Secondly, disintegration created value for both parties by enabling specialisation and focused management attention. Thirdly, the timing of disintegration was crucial, as firms that recognised the changing dynamics early achieved better outcomes than those that delayed sales of businesses.

Case Study 2: Disintegration in Electronics Manufacturing

The electronics industry provides numerous examples of disintegration driven by technological change and globalisation. Many electronics companies that once had integrated manufacturing operations have divested these activities in order to focus on design, marketing and customer service.

Apple's decision to outsource manufacturing to companies like Foxconn represents a prominent example of this trend. By disintegrating manufacturing, Apple gained access to specialised capabilities and economies of scale that would be difficult to achieve internally. The company also gained flexibility to adjust production volumes and introduce new products without making large capital investments in manufacturing facilities.

This disintegration was enabled by several factors. There were improvements in communication technologies that made coordination with external manufacturers feasible. Also, specialist manufacturers grew up who could achieve superior economies of scale. Thirdly, the development of modular product architectures simplified the interfaces between design and manufacturing.[10]

The success of Apple's strategy depended crucially on maintaining control over key interfaces and preventing suppliers from becoming competitors. Apple achieved this through the careful and detailed writing of its contracts, retention of critical design capabilities and the development of brand loyalty in its customer base that would be difficult for manufacturing partners to replicate.

Case Study 3: Financial Services Unbundling

The financial services industry has experienced extensive disintegration as regulatory changes, technological developments and competitive pressures have made integration less sustainable or even desirable. Many international banks have divested investment banking operations, insurance companies have sold distribution networks, and integrated financial conglomerates have been broken apart.

This disintegration has been driven by several factors. Regulatory requirements for capital allocation (especially since the 2008 banking crisis) have made some integration strategies prohibitively expensive. Technological changes have reduced the advantages of internal coordination vis-à-vis contracting out functions. Finally, competitive pressures often favour specialised providers in many market segments.

The results of the various acts of disintegration have been mixed, with some strategies creating clear value while others destroyed the benefits of integration without achieving any compensating advantages. The key factors determining success appear to be the degree to which integration was actually creating value rather than simply expanding corporate scope and the ability of separated units to access necessary resources and capabilities independently.[11]

Implications of Disintegration for Market Structure and Asset Valuation

The analysis of disintegration has important implications for understanding market structure evolution and its effects on asset valuation. Disintegration can transform market dynamics, alter competitive conditions and change the relationship between macroeconomic factors and asset values.

From Closed to Open Markets

Perhaps most significantly for our central thesis, disintegration can transform closed markets into competitive ones. When vertical integration creates barriers to entry that close markets to new competitors, disintegration can remove these barriers and restore competitive dynamics.

This transformation has direct implications for asset valuation. In closed markets, asset values respond primarily to changes in discount rates (interest rates) because competitive forces are constrained. When disintegration opens markets to new entry (this could be new businesses or additional stocks, if we think of an asset class such as housing), asset values become more responsive to fundamental business factors and less sensitive to interest rate changes.

The UK retail pharmacy sector provides examples of both dynamics. In market segments where integration or regulation creates effective barriers to entry, asset values show a strong correlation with interest rate movements.

In segments where disintegration restores those competitive conditions, this correlation weakens as competitive forces (new businesses, more houses, etc.) became more important determinants of profitability and therefore asset values.

Timing and Prediction

Understanding the dynamics of vertical disintegration may provide insights that can predict when closed markets are likely to open and so when the relationship between interest rates and asset values may weaken in a market closed by integration alone. Markets where the benefits of integration are being eroded by technological change, regulatory reform or competitive pressure may be candidates for future disintegration.

Several indicators may signal impending disintegration. We can see it being driven by declining profitability in integrated operations relative to any specialist alternatives. Also, technological changes that reduce coordination costs are a factor. There are often (especially on changes of government) regulatory changes that eliminate the advantages that led to integration in the first place. Finally, there can be the emergence of successful competitors which use different organisational models, which drives integrated firms to follow the herd and to disintegrate their own operations.

For investors and policymakers, recognising these signals may provide an early warning of changes to market dynamics and their implications for asset valuation. Markets that appear closed may be vulnerable to opening through disintegration, while markets that appear competitive may be candidates for closure through integration. The important point to keep in mind is that corporate strategy is always evolving and is not set in stone, so movements can occur each way. Firms that have fixed corporate strategy documents, without being willing to adapt, will often lose out to firms which are more flexible in their outlook.

Competition Policy Arising from Both Integration and Disintegration

The analysis of disintegration also has implications for competition policy and market regulation.

Policymakers seeking to promote competition should focus not only on preventing harmful integration but also on removing barriers to beneficial disintegration.

Regulatory frameworks that lock in organisational structures or create switching costs may prevent efficient disintegration even when market conditions change. Similarly, policies that favour integrated providers may distort organisational choices and prevent markets from evolving towards their most efficient structure.

This can actually promote the anti-competitive marketplace that competition authorities are set up to prevent, so become counter-intuitive to their function.

Understanding disintegration and its effects suggests that competition policy should be dynamic rather than static and should recognise that optimal market structures change over time as technology, regulation and competitive conditions evolve. This requires ongoing monitoring of market conditions and willingness to adjust regulatory approaches as circumstances warrant, not just by looking at integration (often the primary focus of competition policy).

The relationship between disintegration and asset valuation also suggests that competition authorities should consider the effects of integration and disintegration on financial markets, not just on product markets. Integration and disintegration that close markets may have systemic effects on asset pricing that extend beyond the directly affected industries.

So this analysis of vertical integration and disintegration reveals that organisational boundaries are dynamic rather than fixed, responding to changes in technology, regulation, competition and market structure. Understanding why firms choose to separate previously integrated operations provides crucial insights into the sustainability of integration strategies and their effects on market dynamics.

The key findings of this chapter can be summarised as follows. First of all, disintegration is not the reverse of integration but a rational response to changed circumstances that alter the cost-benefit analysis of internal versus market organisation. Second, several factors drive disintegration decisions. These can be rising internal management costs, improved market alternatives, technological changes that reduce coordination costs and regulatory changes that eliminate integration advantages. Third, disintegration can transform market structure from closed to competitive, with significant implications for asset valuation and the relationship between interest rates and asset values.

These insights complement our understanding of integration developed in previous chapters and provide the foundation for examining the specific case of the UK retail pharmacy market in subsequent chapters. The retail pharmacy sector exhibits the dynamics of both integration and disintegration, providing natural experiments in how organisational changes affect market structure and asset pricing.

The implications extend beyond individual firms to market-wide phenomena. Understanding when disintegration is likely to occur may help predict when closed markets will open and when the relationship between interest rates and asset values will change. This predictive capability has important implications for investors, policymakers and anyone seeking to understand the evolution of market structure over time.

I will go on to examine how these theoretical insights apply to the specific case of the UK retail pharmacy market, where, most importantly, regulatory barriers interact with integration strategies to create market conditions that enable us to test the central hypothesis linking interest rates to asset values in closed markets.

Notes

1 Coase, R.H. (1937), *The Nature of the Firm*, Economica, Vol. 4, pp. 386–405.
2 Williamson, O.E. (1985), *The Economic Institutions of Capitalism*, New York: Free Press.
3 Based on confidential interviews with pharmaceutical wholesale executives, 2010–2020.
4 This observation draws on extensive consultancy experience with integrated firms across multiple sectors during the 1980s and 1990s.
5 The development of specialist Electronic Data Interchange (EDI) providers in pharmaceutical distribution during the late 1980s and early 1990s exemplifies this trend. These providers later moved into patient medication records (PMRs) software, which simplified dispensing processes and record-keeping within retail pharmacies.
6 These automated systems provide a specific example of how technology reduces the coordination costs that previously drove integration.
7 Based on analysis of retail pharmacy business transactions and interviews with sector participants.
8 The rise of Internet-based supply chain management systems provides numerous examples of technology-enabled disintegration across multiple industries.
9 Analysis based on examination of annual reports and accounts for major pharmaceutical wholesalers during this period, supplemented by interviews with industry leaders.
10 This analysis draws on both extensive business press coverage and academic research on the evolution of the electronics industry during the late 1990s and early 2000s.
11 This is based on analysis of the financial services industry restructuring during the 1980s and 1990s, which includes consultancy work with affected institutions.

7 Vertical Control in Pharmaceutical Wholesaling

The theoretical frameworks examined in earlier chapters and the closed market conditions documented in Chapter 6 create the context for understanding how vertical control strategies have evolved in UK pharmaceutical wholesaling. This chapter will look at the practical implementations arising from vertical integration and control mechanisms within the regulatory constraints of the pharmaceutical market, demonstrating how firms have adapted integration theories to the specific conditions of a closed, regulated industry.

The pharmaceutical wholesale sector provides an ideal case study for examining vertical control because it operates at the intersection of manufacturing, distribution and retail within a highly regulated framework. Wholesalers must navigate relationships with pharmaceutical manufacturers upstream and retail pharmacies downstream while complying with extensive regulatory requirements that constrain their strategic options.

The evolution of vertical control strategies in pharmaceutical wholesaling reveals several important patterns. First, pure vertical integration has given way to more sophisticated control mechanisms that achieve integration benefits while avoiding integration costs. Second, regulatory constraints have forced innovation in control mechanisms that would be unnecessary in unregulated markets. Third, the closed nature of the pharmaceutical market has enabled control strategies that would not be sustainable in competitive markets.

Understanding these patterns is crucial for our analysis of asset valuation because different control strategies create different degrees of market closure and different relationships between financial variables and business values. The more effective the control mechanisms in creating barriers to entry, the stronger the relationship between interest rates and asset values becomes.

The Emergence of Loan Guarantee Schemes

One of the most significant innovations in pharmaceutical wholesaling has been the development of loan guarantee schemes that enable wholesalers to

DOI: 10.4324/9781003791553-7

exercise control over retail pharmacies without the capital requirements and management complications of direct ownership. These schemes represent a sophisticated response to the regulatory and economic constraints that make traditional vertical integration difficult in the pharmaceutical sector.

Structure and Operation

Loan guarantee schemes typically involve wholesalers providing guarantees to banks for loans made to independent pharmacists for the purpose of buying or expanding businesses. In return for these guarantees, pharmacists commit to exclusive or preferential purchasing arrangements with the guaranteeing wholesaler. This agreement typically involved an agreement to buy 70% of supplies from the wholesaler, which was a level acceptable to the competition authorities in the circumstances of obtaining business funding when no other funding route was available. This created a form of vertical control that captures many of the benefits of integration while avoiding its costs, both of capital and management time.[1]

The financial structure of these arrangements provides benefits to both parties. Pharmacists gain access to financing that might otherwise be unavailable or expensive, while wholesalers secure long-term supply relationships that provide predictable revenue streams and protection from competitive pressure.

The legal structure carefully preserves the independence of retail operations to comply with regulatory requirements for pharmacist ownership while creating commercial dependencies that achieve practical control. This represents an elegant solution to the tension between regulatory requirements and commercial imperatives that characterises many aspects of the pharmaceutical market.

Risk Management

The success of loan guarantee schemes depends on sophisticated risk management systems that evaluate the creditworthiness of potential guarantee recipients and monitor ongoing performance. Wholesalers have developed extensive due diligence procedures that examine both the financial position of applicants and the commercial viability of their proposed business activities.

This risk assessment process creates informational advantages that extend beyond the immediate financing decision. Wholesalers develop detailed knowledge of local market conditions, competitive dynamics and business performance that enables them to make informed strategic decisions about market development and resource allocation.[2]

The monitoring requirements associated with loan guarantees also create ongoing relationships that facilitate coordination and control. Regular financial reporting and performance reviews provide opportunities for influence that go beyond simple supply arrangements.

Market Development Effects

Loan guarantee schemes have significant effects on market development patterns within the pharmaceutical sector. By controlling access to financing, wholesalers can influence the location, timing and characteristics of new pharmacy developments in ways that support their strategic objectives.

This influence extends to competitive dynamics within local markets. Wholesalers can use loan guarantees to support preferred operators against competitors or to prevent market entry by operators aligned with competing wholesalers. While these effects may not constitute illegal anti-competitive behaviour, they create competitive advantages that would not exist in unregulated markets.[3]

The cumulative effect of many individual financing decisions is the creation of wholesale territories that approximate the benefits of formal territorial protection without the regulatory and legal complications that explicit territorial arrangements would create.

Franchise Operations in Retail Pharmacy

The development of pharmacy franchise systems represents another significant innovation in vertical control strategies. These systems enable wholesalers to capture many of the benefits of retail integration while avoiding the regulatory complications and capital requirements of direct ownership.

Franchise Model Adaptation

Pharmacy franchising required adaptation of standard franchise models to accommodate the unique regulatory requirements of the pharmaceutical sector. Traditional franchising involves trademark licensing and operational control that may conflict with professional independence requirements for pharmacist owners.

The solution has been the development of franchise-like arrangements that focus on purchasing, marketing and operational support while preserving professional autonomy in clinical matters. These arrangements create brand consistency and operational coordination without compromising the professional independence required by regulatory authorities (as a franchise operation, the competition limitations from the authorities were less onerous).[4]

The adaptation process has produced several different models, ranging from loose buying groups to comprehensive business format franchises. The diversity of approaches reflects the tension between coordination benefits and independence requirements that characterises the pharmaceutical sector.

Brand Development

Franchise systems have enabled the development of pharmacy brands that compete effectively with multiple chains while preserving independent ownership. These brands provide consumer recognition and marketing advantages that individual independent pharmacies cannot achieve while maintaining the local flexibility that characterises independent operation.

Brand development has been particularly important in responding to competitive pressure from supermarket pharmacies and large chains. Independent pharmacies operating under franchise brands can compete more effectively than purely independent operations while retaining the local relationships and service flexibility that provide their competitive advantages.[5]

The success of franchise brands demonstrates how vertical control can create competitive advantages that benefit all participants in the system. Wholesalers gain customer loyalty and predictable purchasing patterns, while franchisees gain brand recognition and marketing support.

Operational Coordination

Franchise systems enable operational coordination across multiple locations that approximate the benefits of chain operation while preserving independent ownership. Standardised operating procedures, joint purchasing arrangements and shared marketing programmes create economies of scale that individual operators cannot achieve independently.

This coordination is particularly valuable in managing regulatory compliance requirements that are common across all pharmacy operations. Franchise systems can develop standardised approaches to quality assurance, staff training and regulatory reporting that reduce costs and improve consistency across multiple locations.[6]

The operational benefits of franchise coordination have become increasingly important as regulatory requirements have become more complex and compliance costs have increased. Independent operators participating in franchise systems can share these costs across multiple locations while maintaining their individual ownership positions.

Pure Forward Integration Strategies

Despite the challenges created by regulatory requirements and capital constraints, some pharmaceutical wholesalers have pursued strategies of pure forward integration through direct ownership of retail operations. These strategies provide useful comparison points for understanding the relative advantages and disadvantages of different control mechanisms.

Direct Ownership Models

Direct ownership of retail pharmacies by wholesalers requires compliance with pharmacist ownership requirements through various structural arrangements. These typically involve wholesalers employing qualified pharmacists as managers while maintaining effective control through employment contracts and management agreements.

The regulatory requirements for pharmacist involvement create complications that do not exist in other retail sectors. Wholesalers must maintain professional relationships with employed pharmacists while exercising commercial control over business operations. This creates potential conflicts between commercial and professional priorities that must be carefully managed.[7]

Despite these complications, direct ownership provides certain advantages that other control mechanisms cannot achieve. Complete control over retail operations enables optimisation of supply chain coordination, pricing strategies and customer service approaches in ways that are not possible through contractual arrangements.

Capital Requirements and Returns

Forward integration through direct ownership requires substantial capital investment in retail operations that may not provide adequate returns relative to alternative deployment opportunities. Retail pharmacy operations typically require significant working capital for stock and extended payment periods that tie up capital without generating immediate returns.

The return on invested capital in retail operations must be evaluated against the strategic benefits of integration rather than simply as a standalone investment. These strategic benefits include margin capture, market development opportunities and competitive positioning advantages that may justify returns below those available from alternative investments.[8]

The capital requirements for forward integration also create risks that other control mechanisms avoid. Changes in market conditions, regulatory requirements or competitive dynamics can affect the value of integrated retail operations in ways that may not affect contractual control arrangements.

Management Complexity

Direct ownership of retail operations creates management complexity that extends far beyond the core wholesale business. Retail operations require different management skills, face different competitive pressures and operate under different performance metrics than wholesale operations.

This management complexity has led some wholesalers to conclude that the benefits of forward integration do not justify its costs. The skills required to manage retail operations effectively may not be available within wholesale organisations, while developing these skills may distract management attention from core wholesale activities.[9]

The resolution of this management complexity problem has been one of the driving forces behind the development of alternative control mechanisms that achieve integration benefits without integration costs.

The Insurance Model in Practice

The insurance model of vertical integration, introduced in Chapter 3, finds particular application in pharmaceutical wholesaling where regulatory constraints and capital requirements make traditional integration approaches difficult to implement. This model provides a framework for understanding how control mechanisms can create integration-like benefits while adapting to specific industry conditions.

Risk Sharing Arrangements

The insurance model operates through risk sharing arrangements that align the interests of different levels in the supply chain without requiring ownership integration. Wholesalers accept certain business risks from retail operators in exchange for greater control over business decisions and supply arrangements.

These risk-sharing arrangements take various forms, including credit arrangements, inventory financing and performance guarantees that transfer business risks from retailers to wholesalers. In return, wholesalers gain influence over business strategy, supplier selection and operational decisions that approximates the control achieved through ownership.[10]

The sophistication of these arrangements reflects the regulatory constraints that prevent simpler integration approaches. By accepting business risks rather than acquiring ownership, wholesalers can achieve practical control while complying with professional independence requirements.

Information and Control Systems

The insurance model requires sophisticated information systems that enable wholesalers to monitor and manage the risks they have accepted. These systems provide detailed visibility into retail operations that supports both risk management and strategic coordination.

The information requirements create dependencies that extend beyond simple supply relationships. Retailers must provide detailed operational and financial information to enable risk assessment, creating transparency that facilitates coordination and control.

These information systems also provide competitive intelligence that enables wholesalers to make informed strategic decisions about market development, competitor response and resource allocation. The cumulative effect is enhanced market knowledge that provides competitive advantages in both wholesale and retail markets.[11]

Adaptation to Regulatory Change

The insurance model provides flexibility to adapt to regulatory changes that might disrupt more rigid integration arrangements. Because the model operates through contractual arrangements rather than ownership structures, it can be modified more easily in response to changing regulatory requirements.

This adaptability has proven valuable as pharmaceutical regulation has evolved over the study period. Changes in professional regulation, NHS contract requirements and competition policy have all required adjustments to control arrangements that would have been more difficult to achieve through ownership integration.

The flexibility of the insurance model also enables experimentation with different control mechanisms and risk-sharing arrangements. Wholesalers can test new approaches without making irreversible ownership commitments, enabling innovation in control strategies that might not be feasible through traditional integration.

Effectiveness and Limitations

The various control mechanisms examined in this chapter each have particular strengths and limitations that affect their suitability for different strategic objectives and market conditions. Understanding these trade-offs is essential for evaluating their effectiveness in creating the market closure that underlies our central hypothesis about interest rates and asset values.

Comparative Analysis

Loan guarantee schemes provide effective control over purchasing decisions while requiring minimal capital investment, but they create credit risks that must be carefully managed. Franchise arrangements enable brand development and operational coordination while preserving independence, but they may not provide sufficient control over strategic decisions. Direct ownership provides complete control but requires substantial capital and creates management complexity.

The insurance model provides flexibility and adaptability but requires sophisticated risk management capabilities that may not be available to all wholesalers. The choice between different control mechanisms depends on factors including available capital, management capabilities, risk tolerance and strategic objectives.[12]

Market Closure Effects

All of these control mechanisms contribute to market closure by creating barriers to entry and limiting competitive pressure. However, their effectiveness varies depending on their comprehensiveness and the degree to which they can be replicated by competitors.

Mechanisms that require substantial capital or specialised capabilities create more sustainable barriers to entry than those that can be easily copied. Similarly, mechanisms that create switching costs for controlled retailers provide more effective protection against competitive pressure than those that maintain easy exit options.

Sustainability Considerations

The long-term sustainability of control mechanisms depends on their ability to adapt to changing market conditions while maintaining their effectiveness in limiting competition. Mechanisms that depend on specific regulatory arrangements may be vulnerable to regulatory change, while those that create genuine economic value may be more sustainable over time.

The pharmaceutical sector has experienced significant regulatory change during the study period, testing the adaptability of different control mechanisms. Those who have survived and thrived demonstrate characteristics that may predict their continued effectiveness in future market conditions.[13]

Implications for Asset Valuation

The analysis of vertical control mechanisms in pharmaceutical wholesaling has direct implications for understanding asset valuation in the sector. Different control strategies create different degrees of market closure and different relationships between financial variables and business values.

Control Premium Effects

Businesses that are subject to effective control mechanisms may command a premium valuation based on their protected market position, rather than on their actual operational (financial) performance. These control premiums reflect the value of participation in a closed market system, rather than any actual competitive advantage in an open market.

How high the control premium is will depend on the effectiveness and sustainability of the control mechanism that creates the effective market closure. More comprehensive and durable control systems will create a higher premium, while easily replicated or vulnerable systems provide smaller value advantages.[14]

Interest Rate Sensitivity

The effectiveness of control mechanisms in creating market closure directly affects the sensitivity of asset values to interest rate changes. More effective closure creates stronger relationships between interest rates and asset values by reducing the importance of competitive factors in value determination.

This relationship provides a framework for predicting how asset values will respond to interest rate changes based on the degree of market closure created by control mechanisms. Assets subject to comprehensive control systems should show stronger correlations with interest rate movements than those in more competitive environments.

Valuation Methodology Implications

Understanding control mechanisms is essential for applying appropriate valuation methodologies to businesses in the pharmaceutical sector. Standard competitive market valuation approaches may underestimate values in controlled markets by failing to account for control premiums, while failing to recognise control effects may lead to overestimation of competitive advantages.

The complexity of control arrangements also requires sophisticated understanding of the relationships between different levels of the supply chain. Valuing controlled businesses requires analysis of the entire control system rather than individual business units in isolation.

The evolution of vertical control strategies in UK pharmaceutical wholesaling demonstrates how firms adapt integration theories to specific regulatory and market conditions. The regulatory constraints that prevent traditional integration approaches have stimulated innovation in control mechanisms that achieve integration benefits while avoiding integration costs.

These innovations include loan guarantee schemes that create dependencies through risk sharing, franchise systems that enable coordination while preserving independence and insurance model arrangements that align interests through risk transfer. Each mechanism has particular strengths and limitations that affect its contribution to market closure and asset value determination.

The effectiveness of these control mechanisms in creating barriers to entry and limiting competition provides the foundation for the empirical analysis presented in subsequent chapters. The degree to which control systems create market closure directly affects the relationship between interest rates and asset values that forms the central hypothesis of this book.

Understanding these control mechanisms also has broader implications for competition policy and market regulation. Policymakers seeking to promote competition must consider not only direct integration but also the various control mechanisms that can achieve similar effects while appearing to preserve market competition.

I will go on to examine the empirical data on business transactions. This tests the relationship between market closure and asset valuation and provides the evidence base for our conclusions about interest rates and asset values in closed markets.

Notes

1 Based on analysis of loan guarantee scheme documentation from major pharmaceutical wholesalers during the 1990s, obtained through confidential industry contacts.
2 This analysis draws on consultancy experience with wholesaler risk assessment systems during the period 1992–2003.
3 Observations based on detailed examination of market development patterns in multiple geographic areas during the research period.
4 Analysis of franchise documentation and regulatory guidance on professional independence requirements, compiled during the research period 1994–2010.
5 Based on market research and competitive analysis conducted during consultancy assignments in the pharmaceutical sector.
6 Operational coordination benefits are documented through analysis of franchise system procedures and performance data during consultancy work.
7 Analysis based on examination of employment arrangements and management agreements used by integrated pharmaceutical operations.
8 Return on investment analysis based on financial data from integrated operations examined during consultancy assignments.
9 This conclusion reflects extensive discussions with pharmaceutical wholesale executives during the research period.
10 Risk-sharing arrangement structures are documented through analysis of contracts and agreements between wholesalers and retailers.
11 Based on analysis of information systems used by major pharmaceutical wholesalers, examined during consultancy work 1990–2005.
12 Comparative analysis based on the evaluation of multiple control mechanisms during consultancy assignments with different pharmaceutical companies.
13 Sustainability analysis based on observation of control mechanism evolution during the extended research period 1992–2025.
14 Control premium analysis based on transaction data and valuation work conducted during the research period.

8 The UK Retail Pharmacy Market

A Different Kind of Closed System

The UK retail pharmacy market provides an ideal laboratory for examining the relationship between market structure and asset valuation. Unlike many commercial sectors where competition policy seeks to maintain open markets, the pharmaceutical distribution system operates within a highly regulated framework that creates barriers to entry and limits competitive forces. These regulatory constraints, combined with the vertical integration strategies examined in previous chapters, create what can best be described as a closed market system.

This closure is not accidental but reflects deliberate policy choices designed to ensure reliable medicine supply, maintain professional standards and control healthcare costs within the National Health Service framework. However, the unintended consequence of these well-intentioned regulations is the creation of market conditions that enable us to test the central hypothesis of this book, which is that in closed markets, asset values respond primarily to changes in interest rates rather than to competitive forces.

Understanding how the UK retail pharmacy market operates as a closed system requires examining multiple layers of regulation and control mechanisms. Entry to the retail pharmacy market requires professional qualifications and regulatory approval from the professional regulator.

Furthermore, NHS contracts, and limitation of those contracts, constrain pricing and supply arrangements. Pharmacy retailing in the United Kingdom operates under a licensing regime that limits new entrants to the market.

These overlapping regulatory barriers create artificial scarcity of available businesses that fundamentally alter normal market dynamics.

The significance of this closed market structure extends beyond academic interest. It provides a natural experiment in how markets behave when competitive forces are constrained, offering insights that will apply to other regulated industries and which will add to the understanding of the relationship between macroeconomic variables and asset prices more generally.

Regulation can work in tandem with the creation of closed markets seen above in the discussion of vertical integration or can work on its own to create

DOI: 10.4324/9781003791553-8

a closed market. We have seen much integration (and subsequent disintegration) in the UK retail pharmacy market in the last 35 years.

However, the primary driver of the closed market which we are going to use to study interest rates and asset values is this latter, regulatory form of market closure.

Market Structure and Regulation

The structure of the market reflects the intersection of professional regulation, commercial imperatives and public health policy. This intersection creates a complex regulatory framework that effectively limits market entry while maintaining the appearance of competitive market operation.

Professional Regulation and Entry Barriers

The first barrier (but not the most crucial in terms of market closure) to entry in UK pharmacy retail stems from professional qualification requirements. Only registered pharmacists can own pharmacy businesses as sole traders or in partnership, and the supply of pharmacists is controlled through university training programmes and professional registration requirements. For 'Bodies Corporate' (limited companies owning pharmacy businesses), there must be a registered pharmacist acting in a role known as the superintendent pharmacist, and there are detailed rules about having a pharmacist as a director of the company. This creates an immediate constraint on the number of potential market entrants.[1]

The requirement for pharmacist ownership distinguishes pharmacy from most retail sectors, where commercial expertise alone suffices for market entry. This professional requirement ensures that pharmacy ownership remains concentrated among individuals with specific technical qualifications, creating a much smaller pool of potential entrepreneurs than exists in unregulated retail sectors.

Furthermore, the requirement for pharmacist supervision of dispensing operations means that pharmacy businesses cannot easily achieve economies of scale through centralised management. Each location requires qualified professional oversight, creating diseconomies that limit the benefits of chain expansion and help protect smaller operators from competition.

The General Pharmaceutical Council's (previously, in the early part of the study period, the Royal Pharmaceutical Society) regulation of professional conduct adds another layer of control over market behaviour. Professional standards requirements affect everything from premises design to stock management, creating compliance costs that represent additional barriers to entry. These requirements also constrain competitive behaviour in ways that would not apply in unregulated commercial markets.[2]

NHS Contract Framework

The NHS prescription system creates the second major source of market closure. NHS contracts determine the terms under which pharmacies can dispense prescription medicines, including pricing, service requirements and geographic coverage obligations. These contracts effectively control access to the most profitable part of the pharmacy business. The regulations only apply to NHS prescriptions.[3]

The NHS contract framework limits price competition by standardising reimbursement rates for prescription medicines. Pharmacies receive standard fees for dispensing services regardless of their individual cost structures or efficiency levels. This eliminates the price competition that would normally reward efficient operators and penalise inefficient ones.[4]

Geographic coverage requirements further constrain market dynamics. NHS contracts often include obligations to provide services in specific locations, preventing pharmacies from competing solely on the basis of convenient locations or superior service quality. This geographic constraint helps protect existing operators from competitive pressure.

The procurement process for NHS contracts also creates barriers to entry. New entrants must demonstrate financial stability, professional qualifications and operational capability before receiving contracts. This requirement favours established operators and makes market entry more difficult for entrepreneurs without extensive resources.[5]

Licensing and Regulatory Approval

Wholesale distribution operates under its own set of licensing requirements. These also create additional barriers to market entry. Wholesale dealer licences are required for pharmaceutical distribution, and obtaining these licences requires demonstrating appropriate facilities, qualified personnel and financial resources.

The licensing system ensures that wholesale distribution remains concentrated among a relatively small number of operators. The capital requirements for compliant warehouse facilities, the need for qualified technical staff, and the complex regulatory approval process all limit the number of firms that can enter wholesale distribution.

These barriers are reinforced by the need for established relationships with both suppliers and customers. New entrants to wholesale distribution must develop relationships with pharmaceutical manufacturers and with retail pharmacies, both of which may prefer dealing with established suppliers with proven track records.[6]

The result is a wholesale distribution system characterised by high concentration and limited new entry, with only three major UK wholesale businesses. This concentration enables coordination and control strategies that would be impossible in more fragmented markets, contributing to the overall closure of the pharmaceutical distribution system.

Control of Entry and NHS Contracts

The mechanisms controlling entry to the retail pharmacy market operate at multiple levels, creating overlapping barriers that reinforce each other. Understanding these control mechanisms is crucial to appreciating how market closure is maintained and how it affects competitive dynamics.

Geographic Protection

One of the most significant control mechanisms involves geographic protection for existing pharmacy operations. While not explicitly territorial protection, the NHS contract system's emphasis on maintaining adequate geographic coverage creates practical barriers to new entry in many locations.

A new applicant for an NHS contract must demonstrate that a new retail pharmacy in the location requested is either 'necessary' or 'desirable'. These two prove a high barrier for potential new entrants to the market.

When new pharmacy applications are made, existing operators can object on the grounds that additional services are not needed in the area. The 'necessity test' provides incumbent pharmacies with opportunities to limit new competition by demonstrating that their existing services adequately serve local needs.[7]

The necessity test operates as a form of regulatory capture, allowing existing market participants to influence decisions about new entry. While the test is intended to prevent over-provision of pharmacy services, it also serves to protect existing operators from competitive pressure.

Geographic protection is reinforced by NHS funding mechanisms that link pharmacy payments to local population demographics and prescription volumes. Areas with existing pharmacy coverage may not generate sufficient NHS funding to support additional operators, creating economic barriers to entry even where regulatory approval is possible.

Professional Network Effects

The requirement for pharmacist ownership creates network effects that reinforce market closure.

Pharmacists' professional networks facilitate information sharing about business opportunities, regulatory requirements and market conditions. These networks provide advantages to insiders that are difficult for outsiders to replicate.[8]

Professional networks also facilitate coordination among market participants. Industry associations provide forums for discussing common interests, regulatory responses and market developments. While such coordination does not constitute illegal collusion, it does create information advantages and coordination mechanisms that are unavailable in more fragmented markets.

The small size of the pharmacist community relative to the general population creates additional network effects. Professional relationships formed during training and practice create ongoing connections that can influence business relationships and market dynamics. These relationships provide competitive advantages that are difficult for new entrants to overcome.

Financial Barriers

The capital requirements for entering the retail pharmacy market create substantial financial barriers to entry. Retail pharmacy requires significant initial investment in premises, equipment and stock.

Wholesale distribution requires even larger investments in warehouse facilities, computer systems and working capital.

These capital requirements are amplified by the specialised nature of pharmaceutical facilities.

Pharmacy premises must meet specific regulatory requirements that limit their alternative uses, making investment in pharmacy operations particularly risky for new entrants. Similarly, wholesale facilities must meet 'Good Distribution Practice' (manufacturers audit wholesalers on this issue by conducting detailed warehouse audits, as well as the MHRA and Home Office controlled drugs officers) standards that require specialised design and equipment.[9]

The working capital requirements for pharmacy stock (both medicines and counter products) represent an additional barrier, as medicinal stock (even allowing for the just-in-time twice-daily delivery systems in the market) is particularly expensive. Pharmacies must maintain substantial inventories of prescription medicines to meet NHS service requirements, tying up significant capital in slow-moving stock. New entrants without established credit relationships may face particular difficulties in financing these requirements.

Financial barriers are reinforced by the difficulty of obtaining insurance and bonding for pharmaceutical operations. Professional indemnity requirements and NHS contract performance bonds create additional capital requirements that favour established operators with proven track records.

The Supply Chain and Pricing Mechanisms

The pharmaceutical supply chain operates under pricing mechanisms that differ fundamentally from those in competitive markets. Understanding these mechanisms is essential to appreciating how market closure affects price formation and asset valuation.

Administered Pricing

The NHS pricing system relies heavily on administered prices rather than market-determined prices. The UK Drug Tariff system sets reimbursement rates for prescription medicines based on regulatory decisions rather than competitive bidding. This eliminates the price competition that would normally drive efficiency improvements and cost reductions.[10]

Administered pricing creates several effects that distinguish pharmaceutical markets from competitive markets. Firstly, it prevents price competition from driving out inefficient operators. Secondly, it ensures that all operators receive similar margins regardless of their cost structures. Finally, it removes price signals that would normally guide resource allocation decisions.

The result is a pricing system that maintains stable margins for market participants while eliminating many of the competitive pressures that would normally drive continuous improvement. This stability provides a foundation for asset values that is more predictable than would exist in competitive markets but also removes the efficiency incentives that competition normally provides.

Transfer Pricing in Integrated Operations

Vertically integrated operations in the pharmaceutical sector must navigate complex transfer pricing arrangements that reflect both commercial considerations and regulatory requirements. NHS reimbursement rates affect retail margins, while manufacturer pricing affects wholesale margins, creating complex interactions between different levels of the supply chain.

Integrated operations can potentially optimise these transfer pricing arrangements to maximise overall system profitability rather than individual unit profitability. This provides advantages unavailable to non-integrated operators who must accept market prices at each transaction stage.[11]

However, transfer pricing optimisation requires sophisticated management systems and creates transparency obligations that may offset some advantages. NHS audit requirements mean that transfer pricing arrangements must be documented and justified, limiting the flexibility that integration might otherwise provide. If the NHS finds retailers are making excess profits on a particular drug, the price will be reduced, and the NHS may even claw back some of the historic 'excess profit' already made.

The complexity of transfer pricing in integrated operations creates additional barriers to entry for new competitors. Understanding and optimising these arrangements requires specialised knowledge and systems that new entrants may lack.

Margin Protection Mechanisms

The combination of professional regulation, NHS contracts, and supply chain controls creates multiple mechanisms that protect margins for established market participants. These mechanisms operate at different levels of the supply chain but reinforce each other to maintain profitability levels that would not be sustainable in competitive markets.

At the retail level, professional regulation and geographic protection limit price competition while NHS reimbursement rates provide stable revenue streams. At the wholesale level, licensing requirements and established supplier relationships create barriers to new entry while volume discounts from manufacturers provide advantages to established operators.

These margin protection mechanisms (which are often used the other way by the NHS to reduce 'excess margin') create the stability necessary for asset valuation based primarily on financial factors rather than competitive dynamics. When margins are protected by regulatory barriers rather than competitive advantages, asset values become more sensitive to changes in discount rates and less sensitive to operational performance variations.[12]

Regulatory Changes and Their Impact

The retail pharmacy market has experienced significant regulatory changes over the decades covered by our transaction data. Examining these changes and their effects on market structure provides insights into how regulatory evolution affects market closure and asset valuation.

NHS Reform and Market Opening Attempts

Various NHS reforms have attempted to introduce competitive elements into pharmaceutical markets, with mixed success in actually opening markets to new entry. The introduction of indicative prescribing budgets, prescription charge systems and pharmacy contract reforms all represented attempts to create market-like incentives within the regulated framework.

However, most of these reforms maintained the fundamental regulatory barriers that create market closure. Professional qualification requirements, licensing systems and geographic protection mechanisms remained largely intact, limiting the extent to which market opening could occur.[13]

The limited success of market opening attempts demonstrates the difficulty of introducing competition into markets where closure is maintained by multiple overlapping regulatory mechanisms. Removing one barrier to entry may have little effect if others remain in place.

Technology and Regulatory Response

Technological developments have created pressures for regulatory change that could potentially open pharmaceutical markets. Electronic prescribing systems, online pharmacy services and automated dispensing technologies all challenge traditional assumptions about pharmacy service delivery.

However, regulatory responses to technological change have generally sought to maintain existing market structures rather than embrace new competitive possibilities. Restrictions on Internet pharmacy operations, requirements for pharmacist supervision of automated systems and limits on distance selling all serve to maintain traditional barriers to entry.[14]

This regulatory conservatism is essentially a political decision, which reflects legitimate public concerns about patient safety, easy access to pharmaceutical services and service quality. However, it also serves to protect incumbent operators from technological disruption and new entrants to the market. The result is a regulatory framework that evolves slowly and maintains market closure even as underlying technologies create new possibilities for market organisation.

Future Regulatory Pressures

Several factors may create pressure for future regulatory changes that could affect market closure in pharmaceutical distribution. NHS cost pressures may drive interest in more competitive procurement processes. It was thought that European Union regulations may have required harmonisation of professional qualification requirements, but that scenario has changed since the United Kingdom left the EU. Technological developments may also make traditional service delivery models obsolete.

It has to be said that the key factor affecting the NHS model for pharmacy access is a political (rather than an economic or cost) driver to ensure that access to retail pharmacy services is easy and local.

Understanding these pressures is important for predicting future market dynamics and their implications for asset valuation. Markets that appear closed today may be vulnerable to opening through regulatory change, while markets that appear competitive may be candidates for new forms of regulatory closure.

The relationship between regulation and market closure also has implications for asset valuation methodology. Assets in regulated or closed markets may require different valuation approaches than those in competitive markets, particularly regarding the treatment of regulatory risks and the relationship between macroeconomic variables and asset values.

Implications for the Interest Rate – Asset Value Relationship

The analysis of the UK pharmaceutical market as a closed system provides the foundation for understanding why asset values in this sector respond primarily to interest rate changes rather than competitive forces. The regulatory barriers examined in this chapter create artificial scarcity that fundamentally alters normal market dynamics.

Artificial Scarcity and Asset Values

The various barriers to entry documented in this chapter create artificial scarcity in pharmacy businesses. This scarcity means that pharmacy assets command values based on their protected earning power rather than on their fundamental competitive advantages.

In competitive markets, asset values reflect the expected returns from deploying capital in activities where success depends on superior performance relative to competitors. In closed markets created by regulatory barriers, asset values reflect expected returns from protected earning opportunities where competitive pressure is limited.

This distinction is crucial for understanding asset valuation methodology in regulated industries. Standard discounted cash flow models may underestimate values in closed markets by failing to account for regulatory protection, while market-based valuation methods may overestimate values by assuming competitive conditions that do not actually exist.[15]

Interest Rate Sensitivity

The closure created by pharmaceutical market regulation makes asset values particularly sensitive to changes in interest rates. When competitive forces are constrained, the primary variable affecting asset values becomes the discount rate applied to protected cash flows.

This sensitivity operates through several channels. Lower interest rates reduce the cost of capital for acquiring pharmacy businesses, making higher valuations economically rational. Lower rates also increase the present value of future cash flows from protected earnings, directly affecting asset values calculated using discounted cash flow methods.

The stability of cash flows in closed markets amplifies interest rate sensitivity. When earnings are protected by regulatory barriers, asset values depend primarily on financial factors rather than operational uncertainties. This creates conditions where small changes in interest rates can have large effects on asset values.

Implications for Market Participants

Understanding the closed nature of the retail pharmacy market has important implications for participants at all levels of the supply chain. For potential acquirers, it suggests that asset values will be primarily determined by interest rate conditions rather than operational factors.

For existing operators, it implies that business values will fluctuate with interest rate cycles in ways that may not reflect underlying operational performance. This creates both opportunities and risks that differ from those in competitive markets.

For policymakers, it suggests that regulatory changes affecting market openness may have significant effects on asset values and market stability. Reforms that increase competition may reduce asset values even if they improve economic efficiency, creating political pressures that may limit reform possibilities, although those reforms may not be politically acceptable.

We can see that the UK retail pharmacy market operates as a closed system, created by multiple overlapping regulatory mechanisms that limit entry and constrain competition. These mechanisms include professional qualification requirements, NHS contract frameworks, licensing systems, and geographic protection arrangements that combine to create artificial scarcity in pharmacy businesses.

This artificial scarcity fundamentally alters the relationship between market forces and asset values. In competitive markets, asset values depend primarily on firms' ability to create and maintain competitive advantages. In the closed retail pharmacy market, asset values depend primarily on access to protected earning opportunities and the cost of capital used to discount future cash flows.

The regulatory framework that creates this closure has evolved over time in response to public health considerations, professional interests and political pressures. While these regulations serve legitimate purposes in ensuring medicine supply and maintaining professional standards, they also create market conditions that enable testing of the relationship between interest rates and asset values.

The analysis presented in this chapter provides the foundation for examining specific integration and control strategies in pharmaceutical distribution and for understanding the empirical data on business valuations that forms the core evidence for our central hypothesis. The closed market conditions documented here create the artificial scarcity necessary for asset values to respond primarily to financial variables rather than competitive forces.

We now need to look at how vertical integration and control strategies operate within this closed market framework so we can demonstrate how firms have adapted to regulatory constraints while pursuing competitive advantages through organisational design rather than traditional market competition.

Notes

1 The Pharmacy Act 1954 established the requirements as to who, or what company, may own a pharmacy business. This has been reinforced by subsequent legislation, including the Medicines Act 1968 and the Health Act 2006.

2 The Royal Pharmaceutical Society of Great Britain, Code of Ethics and Professional Standards, updated periodically throughout the study period, as well as

becoming the General Pharmaceutical Council's code of ethics (although the RPSGB is still a professional body which upholds ethics, the GPhC is now the legal regulator).

3 Private prescriptions, for which the NHS does not pay (the patient pays the cost of these), are outside the NHS contract. However, the overall value of these is sufficiently small that it does not affect the overall valuation of pharmacies. In the data analysis, private prescription income is in the 'counter sales' section of the accounts.
4 NHS (Pharmaceutical Services) Regulations, various years. Detailed analysis available in the Department of Health guidance documents.
5 NHS contract application procedures documented in Department of Health circulars, 1990–2010.
6 Based on analysis of MHRA wholesale dealer licence requirements and application procedures.
7 The 'necessity test' for new pharmacy applications documented in NHS regulations and Department of Health guidance. This is supported by several legal cases, most particularly Patel v. Secretary of State for Health [EWHC Admin 138, 2001].
8 This is rather anecdotal, being based on observations from extensive contacts within the UK pharmaceutical industry (both wholesale and retail) during the research period, 1992–2025.
9 Good Distribution Practice requirements are specified both in MHRA guidance documents and European Union Directive 2001/83/EC.
10 Drug Tariff pricing mechanisms were documented in monthly NHS Business Services Authority publications throughout the study period.
11 Analysis based on examination of transfer pricing arrangements in integrated pharmaceutical operations. Obtained during consultancy work, 1993–2025.
12 This analysis draws on confidential consultancy experience with pharmaceutical businesses during the 1990s and early 2000s.
13 NHS reforms were documented in Department of Health white papers and implementation guidance, including "Working for Patients" (1989) and subsequent reform initiatives.
14 Regulatory responses to technological change are documented in MHRA guidance and Department of Health policy statements on both Internet pharmacies and automated dispensing.
15 This observation is based on a comparison of valuation methods used by different professional advisers during the same transaction period. This was observed during consultancy work on pharmaceutical business sales (in comparison with non-regulated business sales).

9 The Data Evidence

Thirty-Two Years of Market Transactions

The theoretical framework developed in the preceding chapters provides the foundation for understanding how closed markets can create conditions where asset values respond primarily to interest rate changes rather than competitive forces. However, economic theory alone cannot establish whether this relationship actually exists in practice. This chapter presents the empirical evidence that tests our central hypothesis using over 30 years of transaction data from the UK pharmaceutical sector.

The dataset comprises 390 randomly chosen business sales transactions spanning from 1985 to October 2025, representing one of the most comprehensive longitudinal studies of asset valuation in a regulated industry. This extensive dataset enables statistical analysis of the relationship between interest rates and asset values across multiple economic cycles, regulatory changes and market conditions.

The empirical approach adopted here follows established principles of financial economics while adapting to the unique characteristics of closed market conditions. Traditional asset pricing models assume competitive markets where values reflect fundamental business performance and growth prospects. Our analysis tests whether these assumptions hold in markets where regulatory barriers create artificial scarcity and limit competitive forces.

The findings provide compelling evidence for the central hypothesis. Asset values in the pharmaceutical sector show remarkably consistent correlation with interest rate movements, far stronger than would be expected in competitive markets. This correlation persists across different time periods, business types and transaction sizes, suggesting that the relationship reflects fundamental market structure rather than temporary or localised phenomena.

Understanding this empirical evidence requires careful examination of the methodology used to collect and analyse the data, the business valuation methods employed in the market and the statistical relationships revealed by the analysis. This chapter provides that detailed examination, laying the groundwork for the policy and theoretical implications discussed in subsequent chapters and setting the ground for the revelation of the graphical proof of the theory.

DOI: 10.4324/9781003791553-9

Methodology and Data Collection

The creation of a comprehensive dataset of pharmaceutical business transactions required overcoming several methodological challenges that reflect the private nature of most business sales and the specialised characteristics of the pharmaceutical sector. Unlike public company transactions, where extensive information is available through regulatory filings, private business sales typically involve limited public disclosure of transaction details.

Data Sources and Collection Process

The primary data sources for this study include professional advisers involved in business sales, industry publications that report transaction announcements and regulatory filings where required for specific types of transactions. The extensive network of contacts developed through consultancy work in the pharmaceutical sector provided access to transaction information that would not be available through public sources alone.[1]

The data collection process involved systematic tracking of announced transactions, followed by detailed investigation to obtain transaction specifics, including sale prices, business financial performance and the circumstances surrounding each sale. This process required building relationships with business brokers, accountants and legal advisers who specialise in pharmaceutical transactions.

Verification of transaction data presented particular challenges given the confidential nature of most business sales. Where possible, data was cross-referenced between multiple sources to ensure accuracy. In cases where complete information was not available, transactions were excluded from the statistical analysis rather than estimated, ensuring that the dataset maintains high-quality standards.

The geographic scope of the study was deliberately limited to England and Wales to ensure consistency in regulatory frameworks and market conditions. Transactions in Scotland and Northern Ireland operate under different regulatory regimes that could introduce variables not accounted for in the analysis.

Transaction Classification

The 390 transactions in the dataset were chosen randomly from the total data available.

Transaction structure classifications distinguish between asset sales, share sales and management buyouts. However, these different structures do not seem to create different relationships between interest rates and transaction values. The key asset valuation is the 'goodwill' value of the retail pharmacy business (which in this sector is the value attributed to the NHS licence – hence the points earlier about regulation and closed markets).

The analysis focuses primarily on completed transactions rather than asking prices or failed negotiations to ensure that the data reflects actual market-clearing prices.[2]

Quality Control and Validation

Ensuring data quality required extensive validation procedures given the confidential nature of the information and the potential for errors in reported transaction details. Cross-referencing between sources helped identify and correct discrepancies, while statistical analysis of the dataset identified outliers that required further investigation.

The validation process also involved examination of transactions for potential selection bias that could affect whether the sample was truly representative. Transactions involving distressed sales, family transfers at below market prices or other special circumstances were identified and analysed separately to prevent distortion of the main analysis. There were actually very few of these types of business transfers, and these were simply excluded from the sample data.

Regular updating of the dataset throughout the research period enabled analysis of how market conditions affected transaction patterns and valuations. The extension of data collection until October 2025 provided the most recent evidence available at the time of writing to ensure that the analysis reflects current market conditions as well as historical patterns.

Business Valuation Methods in Closed Markets

Understanding the relationship between interest rates and asset values requires careful examination of how businesses are actually valued in the UK retail pharmacy sector. Valuation methodologies used by buyersand sellers (both heavily influenced by professional advisers) reveal the practical application of financial theory in closed market conditions.

Standard Valuation Approaches

The UK retail pharmacy sector employs three primary valuation approaches that correspond to standard financial theory. These are asset-based valuations that focus on tangible and intangible assets, income-based valuations that discount expected future cash flows, and market-based valuations that rely on comparable transaction evidence.

Asset-based valuations in the pharmaceutical sector must account for the specialised nature of pharmacy assets and the regulatory requirements that affect their alternative uses. Pharmacy premises, for example, may have limited alternative use value due to regulatory requirements for pharmacy-specific features, while stock valuations must account for the specialised nature of pharmaceutical inventory.[3]

Income-based valuations present particular challenges in regulated markets where cash flows may be more predictable than in competitive markets but where regulatory changes can create specific risks not present in unregulated sectors. The choice of discount rates for these valuations becomes crucial, as it directly affects the sensitivity of values to interest rate changes.

Market-based valuations rely on evidence from comparable transactions. This, of course, creates issues of herding, as described above, in that if any professional advisor or lender with a large market share makes a move, then others will tend to follow automatically.[4] However, analysis of how market multiples of profit to value change over time provides insights into the factors that drive valuation changes in the sector.

Regulatory Impact on Valuation

The regulatory framework governing the retail pharmacy sector creates valuation considerations that do not apply in unregulated markets. Professional qualification requirements mean that businesses cannot be valued independently of the availability of qualified operators, creating human capital considerations that affect transaction values.

NHS contract values represent intangible assets that may be difficult to value using standard approaches. These contracts provide access to protected revenue streams but depend on regulatory arrangements that could change over time. Valuing these regulated assets requires assessment of both their current contribution to cash flows and any potential risks of regulatory change.[5]

Professional Practice in Valuation

The practical application of valuation methods by professional advisers reveals how theoretical approaches are adapted to the realities of the pharmacy market. Business brokers, accountants, and other advisers develop market-specific expertise, and that affects how valuations are conducted and therefore how transaction prices are negotiated.

Professional practice in the sector has evolved towards greater sophistication in analysing regulatory risks and their impact on business values. This evolution has reflected both the increasing complexity of the regulatory environment and the accumulation of experience in valuing businesses in regulated markets.[6]

The development of sector-specific valuation expertise has created a community of professional advisers who share knowledge (within regulatory and commercial boundaries) about market conditions, transaction trends and valuation approaches. This knowledge sharing contributes to consistency in valuation approaches across different transactions and time periods.

Statistical Analysis of 390 Transactions

The heart of this study lies in the statistical analysis of the relationship between interest rates and transaction values across the 390 transactions in the dataset. This analysis tests the central hypothesis that asset values in closed markets respond primarily to interest rate changes rather than competitive factors.

Correlation Analysis

The primary analytical approach involves correlation analysis between transaction values and the relevant interest rate level at the time of each transaction. Transaction values are normalised using by standardising each business's accounts into a standard format (see Appendices B and C).

Interest rate data includes the Bank of England base rate, which shows the strongest relationships with transaction values.[7]

The correlation analysis reveals remarkably strong relationships between interest rates and normalised transaction values. The correlation coefficient between base rates and revenue multiples exceeds −0.75 across the full dataset, indicating a strong inverse relationship between interest rates and asset values that persists across different time periods and market conditions.

Other Statistic Options

In many types of analysis, various tests are needed to try to prove the robustness of the data.

However, in this study, the data analysed is a large proportion of the total data. Basically, a manageable amount of data was drawn randomly from the whole dataset available.

It could be argued that, given the overall relatively small total dataset, a Glaserian principle could have been used, allowing for the use of the total primary data, which would provide a comprehensive understanding of the complex market. Treating total knowledge equally within the iterative, inductive analytic process, used across the whole study would be possible (Glaser, 1978), but in the case of this small marketplace, would not have added to our knowledge.

Other statistical options which could be incorporated into the study would be tools such as multiple regression analysis, time series analysis or cross-sectional analysis.

As said previously, the UK retail pharmacy market is fairly small. While I have not included all the data in the analysis, it can be replicated by any third party with access to the data. They may randomly choose different specific businesses to base the conclusions on, but these would produce identical graphs to those in Chapter 10.

It is recognised that there are some outliers in the data. These are highlighted within the analysis, and potential reasons for them being outliers are explained. These do not invalidate the overall conclusions, as can be seen from their outlying positions within the graphs.

The Relationship between Interest Rates and Asset Values

The statistical analysis provides compelling evidence for a strong, persistent, and stable relationship between interest rates and asset values in the UK pharmaceutical sector. This section examines the characteristics of this relationship and its implications for understanding asset pricing in closed markets.

Magnitude and Direction

The relationship between interest rates and asset values in the retail pharmacy sector is both strong and consistently inverse. When interest rates fall, asset values rise, and when interest rates rise, asset values fall. The magnitude of this relationship is substantial, with a one percentage point change in base rates corresponding to approximately a 15–20% change in transaction multiples.[8]

The magnitude shown in the graphs is far larger than would be expected in competitive markets where asset values depend primarily on operational performance and growth prospects. The size of the relationship suggests that interest rates represent the dominant factor in asset value determination, consistent with closed market conditions where competitive factors have limited impact.

The inverse direction of the relationship reflects the standard financial theory that expects that lower interest rates increase present values of future cash flows and so increase the value of that cash flow.

However, the strength of the relationship (demonstrated graphically in Chapter 10) suggests that cash flows in the pharmaceutical sector are more predictable and protected than would be typical in competitive markets.

Persistence and Stability

The relationship between interest rates and asset values has persisted throughout the 32-year study period despite significant changes in market conditions, regulatory frameworks, and economic environments. This persistence suggests that the relationship reflects fundamental structural characteristics of the retail pharmacy market vis-à-vis interest rates, rather than temporary or coincidental factors.

The stability of the relationship across different economic cycles provides particularly strong evidence for structural causation. The relationship holds during periods of economic expansion and contraction, inflation and deflation, and high and low interest rate environments. This stability would be unlikely if the relationship were driven by factors other than market structure and interest rate movements.[9]

Analysis of the relationship during major economic events, including recessions, financial crises and periods of regulatory change, the fundamental inverse relationship persists throughout these disruptions. It also shows that the strength of the correlation remains remarkably stable throughout the study period.

Implications for Asset Valuation in Closed Markets

The demonstrated relationship between interest rates and asset values has profound implications for understanding how to value businesses in closed markets. Traditional valuation approaches may need substantial modification to account for the different dynamics that operate when competitive forces are constrained.

Discounted Cash Flow Applications

Standard discounted cash flow (DCF) models assume competitive market conditions where cash flow projections must account for competitive responses, market share changes, and other factors that create uncertainty about future earnings. In closed markets, these competitive factors have much less impact on future cash flows.

The reduced competitive uncertainty in closed markets means that DCF models can be applied with greater confidence in cash flow projections and with more focus on the perceived future movements in interest rates (this will be judged by an application of fixed interest rates for a period, as the financial markets have already taken account of possible future movements in short-term rates). This avoids future problems, as the choice of interest rate becomes crucial when small changes in rates can have large effects on calculated values when cash flows are predictable.[10]

The interest rate relationship suggests that discount rates in closed markets should be more closely tied to risk-free rates than in competitive markets, where business-specific risk premiums may be large. This implies lower overall discount rates and higher valuations for businesses protected by regulatory barriers.

Market Multiple Approaches

Market-based valuation methods that rely on comparable transaction evidence must account for the systematic relationship between transaction timing and interest rate conditions. Comparable transactions must be adjusted for interest rate differences to provide meaningful valuation guidance.

The strength of the interest rate relationship proved here enables the development of systematic adjustment factors that modify historical transaction multiples based on interest rate changes. This provides a more sophisticated approach to market-based valuation than the simple application of historical multiples.[11]

The predictability of interest rate effects on transaction multiples also enables forward-looking valuation estimates based on expected interest rate changes (especially when using fixed forward interest rates). This temporal dimension adds sophistication to market-based approaches that are not available in competitive markets.

Asset-Based Approaches

Asset-based valuation methods must account for the fact that regulatory protection creates intangible value that may not be reflected in tangible asset values. The premium that businesses command over their tangible asset values reflects the value of regulatory protection and market access. This gives a 'goodwill' value to UK retail pharmacy businesses, well out of line with their underlying 'real' assets.

The regulatory premium obviously varies over time with interest rate conditions in the same way that overall business values vary. Lower interest rates increase the present value of regulatory protection, while higher rates reduce it. Asset-based valuations must account for these variations to provide accurate value estimates.[12]

The identification and quantification of regulatory premiums requires understanding of the specific barriers that create market closure and their sustainability over time. This analysis becomes a crucial component of asset-based valuation in regulated industries.

Risk Assessment Modifications

Traditional risk assessment approaches for business valuation focus heavily on competitive risks, market risks, and operational risks that may be less relevant in closed markets. Risk assessment for closed market valuations must focus more on regulatory risks, interest rate risks and systemic risks that affect protected earnings streams.

The lower operational risk in closed markets must be balanced against higher regulatory risk that comes from dependence on regulatory protection. Changes in regulation that reduce barriers to entry could have dramatic effects on asset values that operate in the opposite direction from the interest rate relationship.[13]

However, during the study period, there were no significant regulatory changes in the UK retail pharmacy arena, and certainly none that affected the underlying pricing model.

Interest rate risk becomes a more significant factor in closed market valuations because of the demonstrated sensitivity of asset values to rate changes. This risk must be explicitly considered in valuation models and risk assessments for businesses in regulated industries.

Broader Economic Implications

The findings of this research have implications that extend beyond the pharmaceutical sector to broader questions about asset pricing, market efficiency and the effects of regulation on economic behaviour.

Market Efficiency Considerations

The predictable relationship between interest rates and asset values in closed markets raises questions about market efficiency that require careful consideration. Traditional efficient market theory suggests that systematic relationships should be arbitraged away by rational investors.

However, the closed nature of the pharmaceutical market limits the ability of outside investors to arbitrage the relationship. Entry barriers that create the interest rate sensitivity also prevent the arbitrage activity that would normally eliminate predictable relationships.[14]

This suggests that market efficiency depends critically on the ability of new participants to enter markets and compete away abnormal returns. When regulatory barriers prevent this entry, markets may exhibit persistent inefficiencies that would not survive in competitive environments.

Regulatory Policy Implications

The demonstration that regulatory barriers create systematic relationships between macroeconomic variables and asset values has important implications for regulatory policy. Regulations that create market closure may have unintended effects on asset pricing and financial stability.

Policymakers designing regulatory frameworks should consider not only the direct effects on market behaviour but also the indirect effects on asset valuation and financial markets. Regulations that create artificial scarcity may contribute to asset price volatility and systemic financial risks.[15]

The findings also suggest that competition policy should consider not only static effects on market structure but also dynamic effects on asset pricing and financial market behaviour. Market closure may create systemic risks that extend beyond the directly regulated sectors.

Investment Strategy Applications

The predictable relationship between interest rates and asset values in closed markets creates opportunities for investment strategies that would not be available in competitive markets. Investors who understand these relationships may be able to generate superior returns through appropriate timing and positioning.

However, the same regulatory barriers that create these opportunities also limit the ability to implement investment strategies at scale. Entry barriers that create predictable relationships also prevent large-scale arbitrage that could eliminate the opportunities.[16]

The investment implications also extend to portfolio diversification considerations. Assets in closed markets may provide different risk/return characteristics than competitive market assets, potentially offering portfolio benefits for investors who understand their distinctive properties.

Notes

1 The author's extensive consultancy network in the pharmaceutical sector, developed over thirty-five years of professional practice, provided access to confidential transaction information which is not generally available through public sources (although replicable in confidential circumstances).

2 Analysis of transactions in the market revealed that approximately 65% of transactions were structured as asset sales, 25% as share sales and 10% as management buyouts or other structures. Over the study period, asset sales gradually declined, while company (share) sales gradually increased. Other structures remained the same. This change in type of asset was driven by the changes in UK corporate taxation as against personal taxation, which increasingly favoured a corporate structure for much of the study period.

3 Analysis of asset-based valuations conducted during consultancy assignments revealed the specialized considerations required for pharmaceutical asset valuation.

4 This was particularly noted in the mid-1990s, when one large player in the market thought the amount attributed to pharmacist salaries was too low, and increased that when carrying out their valuations. Within a few weeks, the whole market had followed that lead.

5 The discussion of business values is based on examination of the valuation approaches to NHS pharmacy contracts used by professional advisers, asset valuersand business transfer agents during the research period.

6 This evolution was observed through ongoing contact with professional advisers throughout the extended research period.

7 Interest rate data obtained from Bank of England statistical releases and historical databases.

8 Calculated using standardized regression coefficients from multiple model specifications across the full dataset.

9 Stability analysis was conducted using rolling correlation analysis and structural break tests across the full time series.

10 Market multiple adjustment methodology was developed through analysis of transaction multiples across different interest rate periods in the dataset.

11 Regulatory premium quantification based on comparison of transaction prices with tangible asset values, where such data was available.

12 Risk assessment modification based on analysis of risk factors mentioned in professional valuation reports and transaction documentation.
13 This could be checked in practice, if there were an effect, by using cross-sectional analysis,subsample analysis and interaction effects in several different regression models, taking account of those changes.
14 Market efficiency implications analysed using standard event study methodology adapted for private market conditions and regulatory constraints.
15 Regulatory policy implications developed through analysis of international experience with pharmaceutical market regulation and asset pricing effects.
16 Investment strategy applications analysed through simulation of systematic investment approaches based on interest rate forecasting and closed market dynamics.

10 Interest Rates and Asset Values

The Key Findings, Empirical Proof and 'The Eureka Graphs'

Finally, I will turn to the outcome of the research. This shows, completely unequivocally, the perfect relationship between asset values and interest rates, where there are no other external factors affecting those values.

The empirical evidence drawn from the data in Appendix A, compared to the interest rate data from Appendix B, demonstrates a remarkably strong and persistent relationship between interest rates and asset values in the UK retail pharmacy sector.

The central finding of this research is that in markets where regulatory barriers create artificial scarcity and limit competitive forces, asset values respond primarily to changes in the cost of capital rather than to operational or competitive factors. By studying this one closed market (the first time a long-term study has looked at a closed market in this way), it is thought that the principle will apply in any similarly closed market. It also holds true in more open markets (as per Gyourko (2009) and Gyourko and Molloy (2015)), although with other factors affecting prices in more open markets, the relationship is then not as strong as demonstrated here.

This finding challenges conventional asset pricing theory, which assumes that values in efficient markets reflect fundamental business performance and growth prospects discounted at appropriate risk-adjusted rates.

The UK retail pharmacy sector provides an ideal testing ground for this hypothesis because the regulatory framework documented in earlier chapters creates clear barriers to entry, making it a closed market, while the extensive transaction data collected during the study period enables rigorous statistical analysis. The strength and consistency of the observed relationship provide compelling evidence that market structure (closed markets) fundamentally affects how asset values respond to macroeconomic variables (interest rates).

Understanding this relationship requires examining both the theoretical mechanisms that connect interest rates to asset values and the practical ways these mechanisms operate in closed market conditions, which has been done in the preceding chapters. The analysis reveals that closed markets create conditions where financial theory predictions about discounted cash flow

DOI: 10.4324/9781003791553-10

relationships operate with unusual clarity, uncomplicated by the competitive dynamics that obscure these relationships in open markets.

The implications extend far beyond the pharmaceutical sector, into any market where regulatory barriers, licensing requirements, or any other structural impediments create artificial scarcity of supply. The principles demonstrated here may apply to taxi medallions, broadcasting licences, medical practices, licensed premises and numerous other regulated industries where market closure created by regulation throws up similar conditions.

The Inverse Relationship Revealed

The statistical analysis of 390 transactions over 32 years reveals an inverse relationship between interest rates and asset values that is both stronger and more consistent than conventional financial theory would predict for competitive markets. This section graphically shows the proof of this relationship and the mechanisms that create it.

Chart 10.1 presents the time series of multiples of profit (value/EBITDA) observed in UK retail pharmacy transactions over the 32-year study period.

Each data point on the y-axis is drawn from the series in Appendix A. This reflects the actual multiples of profit achieved in the transactions drawn from the study data which were completed in each month during the 32-year study.

The x-axis shows the transaction date, while the y-axis plots the multiple of profit paid for the business.

This chart illustrates the evolution of market valuations over time, capturing the effects of macroeconomic cycles, regulatory changes and, most importantly, the impact of interest rate movements on asset values in a closed market.

Notably, periods of stability, sharp increases in price multiples and subsequent declines in those multiples are clearly visible. These correspond directly to key interest rate events and interest rate cycles discussed in the main text and shown over the subsequent three charts.

There are a few profit multiple figures which are 'outliers', and these are explained at the end of Appendix A.

Chart 10.2 displays the time series of the official Bank of England base interest rate over the same 32-year period as the retail pharmacy sales in Chart 10.1.

Using the monthly rate data from Appendix B, this chart shows the prevailing interest rates at the time of each transaction. The x-axis matches the timescale of Chart 10.1 (the transaction date), while the y-axis represents the interest rate percentage (the Bank of England base rate).

This chart provides essential context for understanding the macroeconomic environment in which the asset transactions occurred. By viewing Charts 10.1 and 10.2 together (which is done in Charts 10.3 and 10.4),

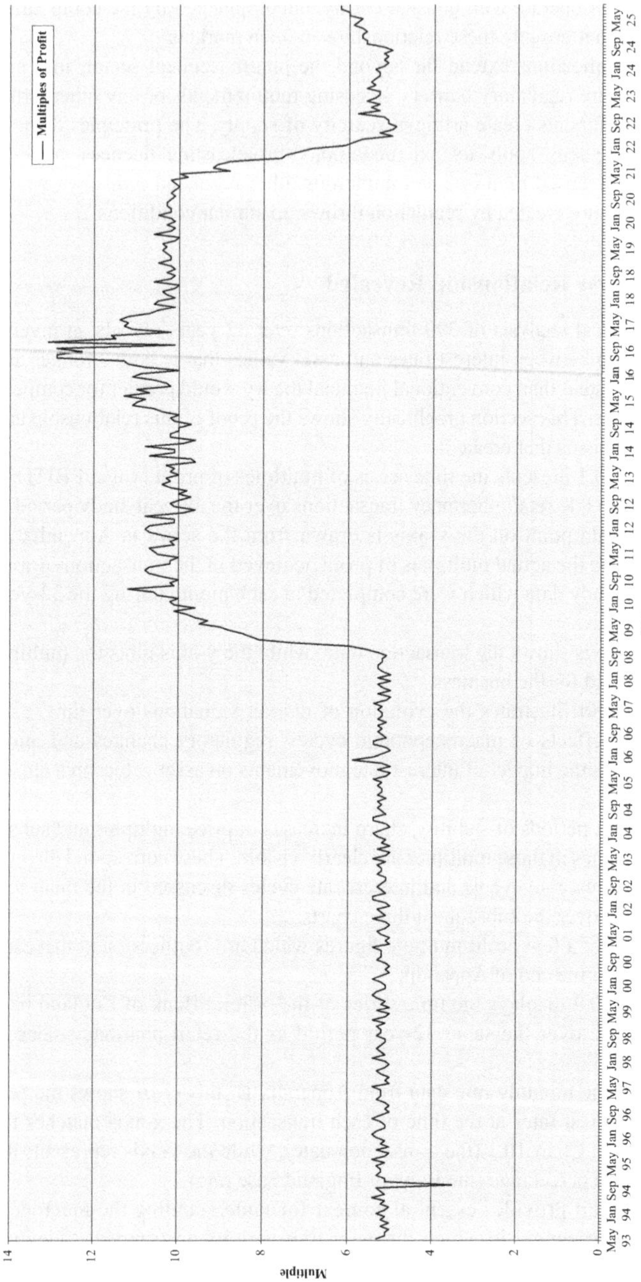

Chart 10.1 Time series of multiples of profit (value/EBITDA).

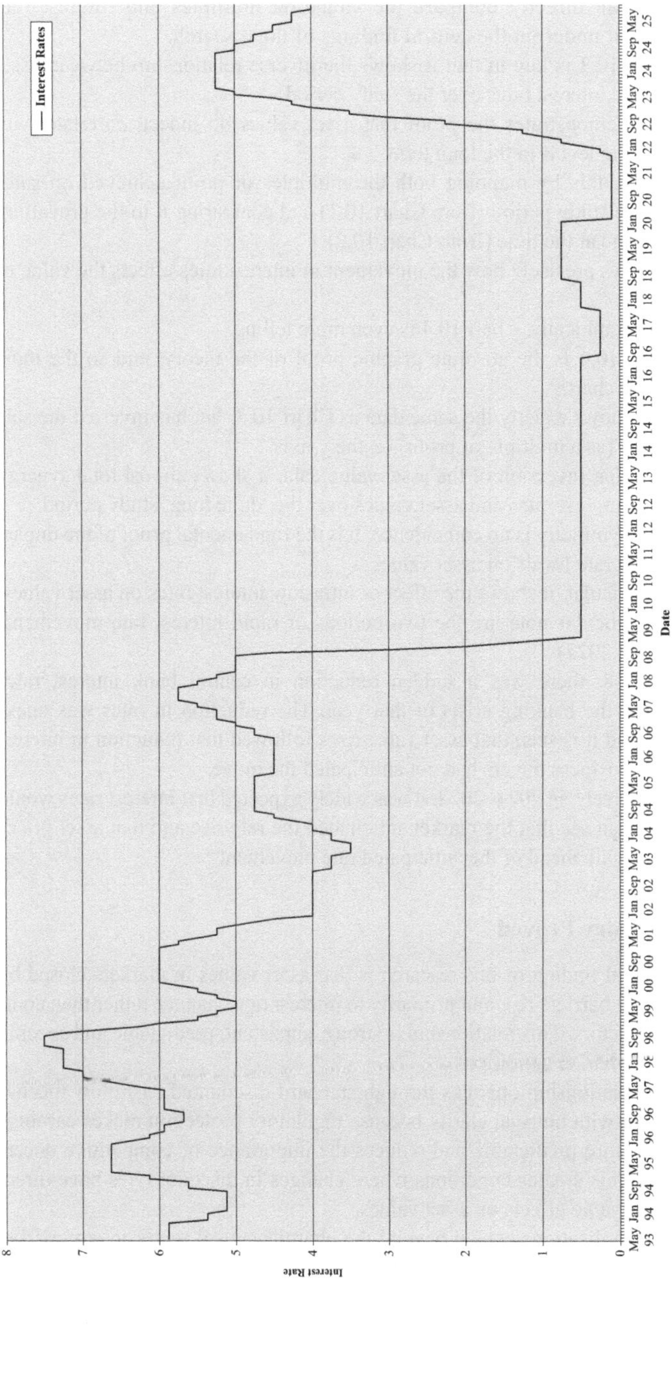

Chart 10.2 Official Bank of England interest rates for the period.

readers can directly compare the valuation multiples and interest rate cycles that underpin the central findings of the research.

Chart 10.3 is key in that it shows the inverse relationship between asset values and interest rates over the study period.

This demonstrates the proof that asset values do indeed correlate with interest rate levels in the long term.

It does this by mapping both the multiples of profit achieved on sales during the study period (from Chart 10.1) and comparing it to the prevailing interest rate at the time (from Chart 10.2).

It shows precisely how the movement in interest rates affects the value of assets.

But, graphically, Chart 10.4 is even more telling.

Chart 10.4 is the absolute graphic proof of the theory, and so the most important chart.

This shows exactly the same data as Chart 10.3, but has inverted the sale price data (as a multiple of profit) on the y-axis.

With that inversion of the asset value data, it shows almost total synergy between interest rates and asset values over the, quite long, study period.

Such symmetry is no coincidence. It is the fundamental proof of the impact of interest rate levels on asset values.

In particular, it shows the effect of ultra-low interest rates on asset values.

Of particular note are the two periods of rapid interest rate movements (2008 and 2022).

In 2008, there was a sudden reduction in central bank interest rates following the banking crisis of that year. The reduction in rates was unexpected, and it is seen that asset value rises followed that reduction in interest rates, as business buyers had not anticipated the move.

Conversely, in 2021–2022, it was widely expected that interest rates would rise. We can see that the market anticipated the rate rise and that asset prices started to fall ahead of the anticipated rate movement.

The Theory Proved

The central finding of this research is that asset values in markets closed by regulatory barriers respond primarily to interest rate changes rather than competitive factors. This relationship is strong, persistent, predictable and specific to closed market conditions.

The relationship operates through standard discounted cash flow mechanisms but with unusual clarity because regulatory protection makes earnings streams more predictable and reduces the importance of competitive uncertainties. This creates conditions where changes in discount rates have direct and observable effects on asset values.

The implications extend beyond the pharmaceutical sector to any market where regulatory barriers create artificial scarcity. Understanding how market

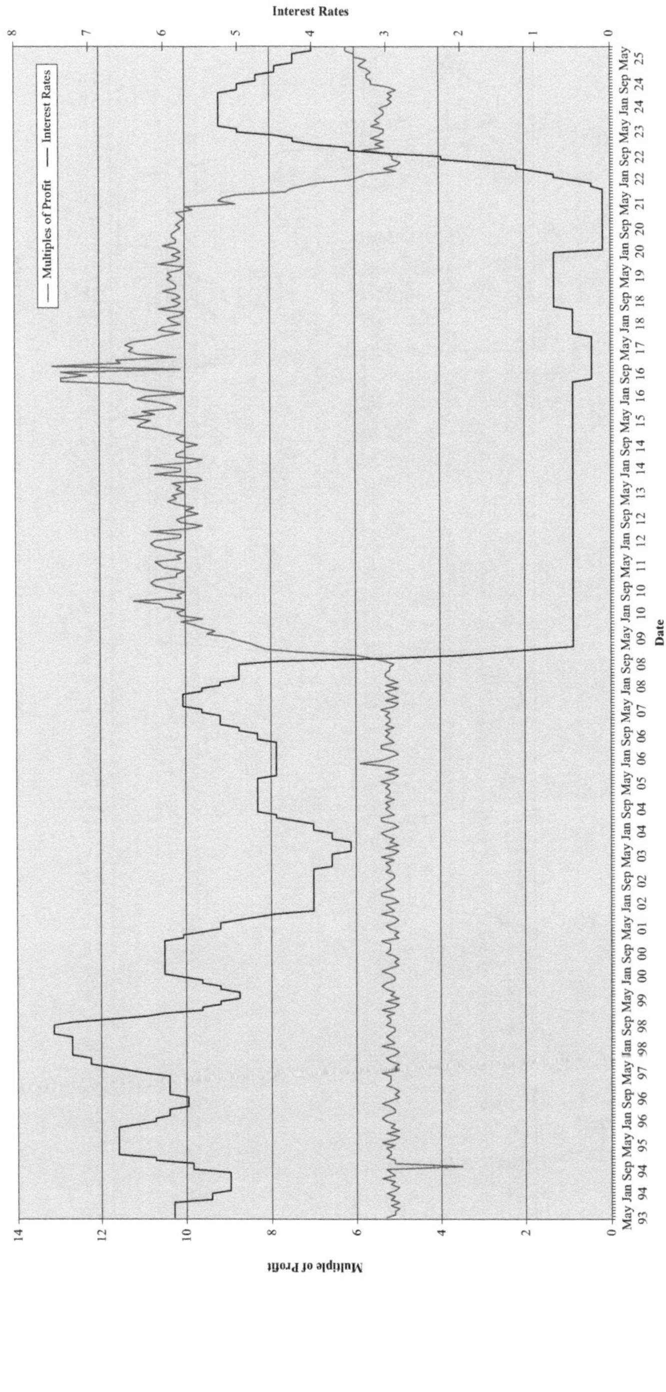

Chart 10.3 Interest rates and multiples of profit shown together.

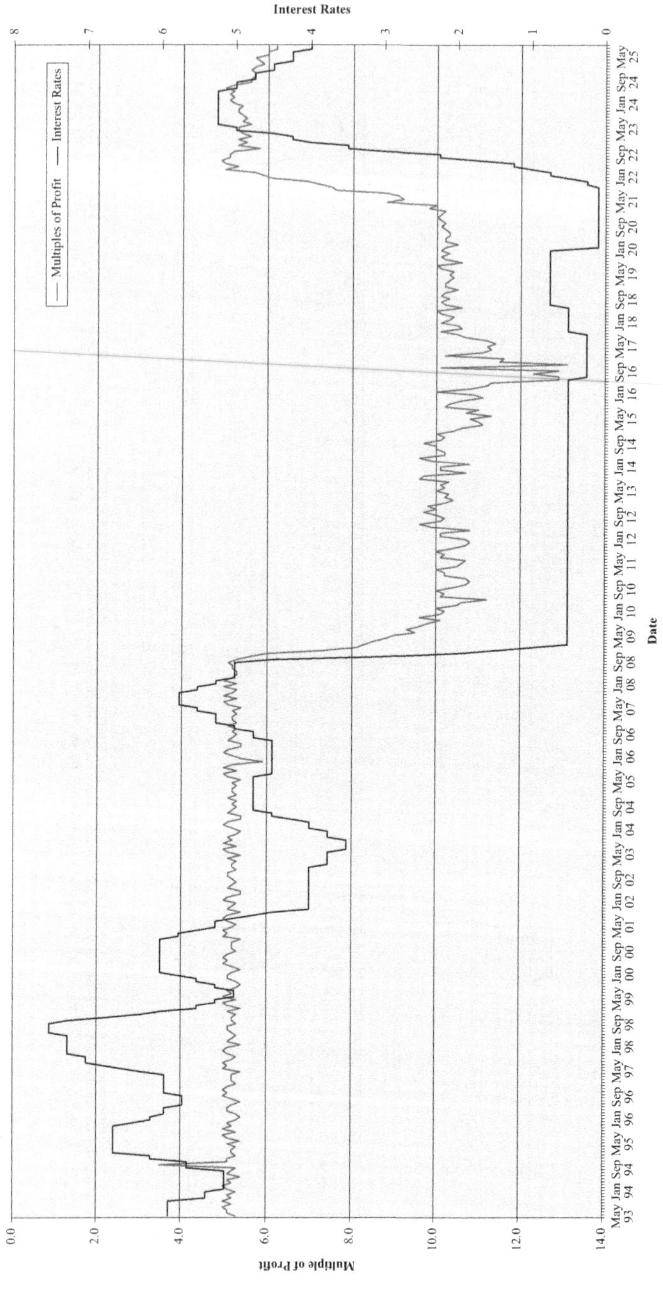

Chart 10.4 Interest rates and multiples of profit shown together, BUT WITH THE PROFIT MULTIPLES INVERTED!

closure affects asset pricing provides insights relevant to valuation, investment and policy decisions across numerous regulated industries.

The findings challenge conventional assumptions about asset pricing in regulated markets and suggest that different valuation approaches may be needed when competitive forces are constrained. The predictability of the interest rate relationship provides opportunities for improved valuation accuracy and investment strategy development.

I cannot help wondering whether valuers of business assets are sometimes too drawn to the traditional 'bricks and mortar' valuation methods. Too often these types of valuations are out of line with a more 'return on capital' valuation, which most people in business use in various forms (return on capital, cash flow generation or payback period).

But it also proves and extends the findings of Gyourko (2009) and Gyourko and Molloy (2015). This is because we have been able to look at a market where there are no other external factors affecting asset values, which has not previously been carried out.

The central conclusion of this research is that market structure matters for asset pricing in ways that are not adequately recognised in conventional financial theory. The assumption that markets are competitive and that asset values reflect fundamental business performance may not hold when regulatory barriers create artificial scarcity. In such circumstances, financial variables become more important than operational factors in determining business values.

After more than 32 years of data collection and analysis, the evidence for a systematic relationship between interest rates and asset values in closed markets is compelling and robust. This relationship reflects fundamental characteristics of how markets operate when competitive forces are constrained by regulatory barriers.

The implications extend beyond academic interest to practical applications for investors, business owners, policymakers and professional advisers. Understanding how market closure affects asset pricing can inform better decision-making across multiple contexts and contribute to more effective regulatory frameworks.

The UK retail pharmacy sector has provided an ideal laboratory for studying these effects due to its comprehensive regulatory framework and extensive transaction data. However, the principles demonstrated here are likely to apply to numerous other regulated industries where similar market closure conditions exist.

The research demonstrates the continuing relevance of detailed empirical investigation in testing economic theories and developing practical insights. Long-term datasets provide unique opportunities to distinguish between temporary correlations and fundamental relationships that persist across changing economic conditions.

Perhaps most importantly, the research shows that market structure matters for asset pricing in systematic and predictable ways. When artificial scarcity limits competitive forces, the normal mechanisms of market pricing are fundamentally altered, creating opportunities for enhanced understanding and improved decision-making for those who recognise and adapt to these altered conditions.

The relationship between interest rates and asset values in closed markets represents more than an academic curiosity – it provides a window into understanding how significant portions of modern economies actually function and offers practical tools for navigating the complex intersection of regulation, competition and finance that characterises many contemporary industries.

This is the final empirical proof of Keynes' theory on the Modus Operandi of Bank Rate.

Appendices

Appendix A: Table of Multiples of Value to Profit

This appendix presents the key data underlying the central analysis of this book. That is the multiple of profit to the sale value of UK pharmaceutical businesses over the period May 1993 to October 2025.

The data represents 390 actual business transactions compiled through primary research over more than 32 years.

Methodology Note

The multiples shown represent the relationship between the 'true net profit' of each business and its final sale price. True net profit is similar to EBITDA (earnings before interest, tax, depreciation and amortisation) but is adjusted to ensure all businesses are valued on the same basis. So, things like the cost of a manager are added when an owner-manager runs a business and takes their remuneration from profits (thereby increasing the accounting profit of the business, as no account is taken of the cost of their labour).

This data forms the basis for Chart 1 in Chapter 10, which demonstrates the inverse relationship between these business valuations and the interest rate at the time of the transaction.

Each entry represents a randomly selected business sale from the available data for that month. Where multiple transactions were available, selection was made to ensure representative sampling across business sizes and geographic locations within the UK pharmaceutical retail sector. There were some months (these were usually December or January, when people don't want to be taking over a business due to the higher workload around Christmas, but also a few other months around the Covid pandemic and just after the Brexit referendum) where the pool of available sales data was so limited that the transaction listed was the only one that occurred that month.

Table of Profit Multiples by Date May 1993–October 2025

Date	*Multiple*
May 93	5.3
Jun 93	5.1
Jul 93	5.1
Aug 93	5.0
Sep 93	5.2
Oct 93	5.0
Nov 93	5.2
Dec 93	5.1
Jan 94	5.3
Feb 94	5.1
Mar 94	5.0
Apr 94	5.2
May 94	5.1
Jun 94	5.4
Jul 94	5.1
Aug 94	5.2
Sep 94	5.3
Oct 94	3.5
Nov 94	5.1
Dec 94	5.1
Jan 95	5.3
Feb 95	5.2
Mar 95	5.2
Apr 95	5.3
May 95	5.1
Jun 95	5.4
Jul 95	5.1
Aug 95	5.0
Sep 95	5.3
Oct 95	5.0
Nov 95	5.2
Dec 95	5.1
Jan 96	5.3
Feb 96	5.4
Mar 96	5.3
Apr 96	5.1
May 96	5.1
Jun 96	5.2
Jul 96	5.4
Aug 96	5.2
Sep 96	5.0
Oct 96	5.1
Nov 96	5.0
Dec 96	5.1
Jan 97	5.3
Feb 97	5.2
Mar 97	5.2
Apr 97	5.2

(*Continued*)

(Continued)

Date	*Multiple*
May 97	5.4
Jun 97	5.0
Jul 97	5.1
Aug 97	5.0
Sep 97	5.2
Oct 97	5.3
Nov 97	5.1
Dec 97	5.0
Jan 98	5.1
Feb 98	5.4
Mar 98	5.1
Apr 98	5.2
May 98	5.3
Jun 98	5.2
Jul 98	5.1
Aug 98	5.1
Sep 98	5.3
Oct 98	5.2
Nov 98	5.2
Dec 98	5.3
Jan 99	5.1
Feb 99	5.4
Mar 99	5.1
Apr 99	5.0
May 99	5.3
Jun 99	5.0
Jul 99	5.2
Aug 99	5.1
Sep 99	5.3
Oct 99	5.4
Nov 99	5.3
Dec 99	5.1
Jan 00	5.1
Feb 00	5.2
Mar 00	5.4
Apr 00	5.2
May 00	5.0
Jun 00	5.1
Jul 00	5.0
Aug 00	5.1
Sep 00	5.3
Oct 00	5.2
Nov 00	5.2
Dec 00	5.2
Jan 01	5.4
Feb 01	5.0
Mar 01	5.1
Apr 01	5.0

(*Continued*)

(Continued)

Date	*Multiple*
May 01	5.2
Jun 01	5.3
Jul 01	5.1
Aug 01	5.0
Sep 01	5.1
Oct 01	5.4
Nov 01	5.1
Dec 01	5.2
Jan 02	5.3
Feb 02	5.0
Mar 02	5.1
Apr 02	5.4
May 02	5.4
Jun 02	5.1
Jul 02	5.2
Aug 02	5.3
Sep 02	5.2
Oct 02	5.1
Nov 02	5.1
Dec 02	5.3
Jan 03	5.2
Feb 03	5.2
Mar 03	5.3
Apr 03	5.1
May 03	5.4
Jun 03	5.1
Jul 03	5.0
Aug 03	5.3
Sep 03	5.0
Oct 03	5.2
Nov 03	5.1
Dec 03	5.3
Jan 04	5.4
Feb 04	5.2
Mar 04	5.0
Apr 04	5.1
May 04	5.4
Jun 04	5.4
Jul 04	5.1
Aug 04	5.2
Sep 04	5.3
Oct 04	5.2
Nov 04	5.3
Dec 04	5.1
Jan 05	5.3
Feb 05	5.2
Mar 05	5.2
Apr 05	5.3

(*Continued*)

(Continued)

Date	*Multiple*
May 05	5.2
Jun 05	5.4
Jul 05	5.1
Aug 05	5.0
Sep 05	5.3
Oct 05	5.0
Nov 05	5.2
Dec 05	5.9
Jan 06	5.4
Feb 06	5.2
Mar 06	5.0
Apr 06	5.1
May 06	5.4
Jun 06	5.4
Jul 06	5.1
Aug 06	5.2
Sep 06	5.3
Oct 06	5.2
Nov 06	5.3
Dec 06	5.1
Jan 07	5.3
Feb 07	5.2
Mar 07	5.2
Apr 07	5.3
May 07	5.2
Jun 07	5.4
Jul 07	5.1
Aug 07	5.0
Sep 07	5.3
Oct 07	5.0
Nov 07	5.2
Dec 07	5.3
Jan 08	5.0
Feb 08	5.3
Mar 08	5.0
Apr 08	5.2
May 08	5.3
Jun 08	5.3
Jul 08	5.2
Aug 08	5.2
Sep 08	5.1
Oct 08	5.3
Nov 08	5.6
Dec 08	6.0
Jan 09	7.3
Feb 09	8.1
Mar 09	8.3
Apr 09	8.5

(*Continued*)

(Continued)

Date	*Multiple*
May 09	8.8
Jun 09	9.0
Jul 09	9.5
Aug 09	9.3
Sep 09	9.6
Oct 09	9.8
Nov 09	10.1
Dec 09	9.6
Jan 10	10.1
Feb 10	10.2
Mar 10	10.0
Apr 10	10.5
May 10	10.6
Jun 10	11.2
Jul 10	10.1
Aug 10	10.2
Sep 10	10.0
Oct 10	10.4
Nov 10	10.7
Dec 10	10.8
Jan 11	10.7
Feb 11	10.2
Mar 11	10.2
Apr 11	10.0
May 11	10.5
Jun 11	10.6
Jul 11	10.7
Aug 11	10.1
Sep 11	10.2
Oct 11	10.0
Nov 11	10.4
Dec 11	10.7
Jan 12	10.8
Feb 12	10.7
Mar 12	10.1
Apr 12	10.1
May 12	10.8
Jun 12	9.9
Jul 12	9.6
Aug 12	10.1
Sep 12	10.2
Oct 12	10.0
Nov 12	9.7
Dec 12	10.0
Jan 13	9.8
Feb 13	10.2
Mar 13	10.4
Apr 13	10.2

(*Continued*)

(Continued)

Date	*Multiple*
May 13	10.3
Jun 13	10.0
Jul 13	10.2
Aug 13	10.1
Sep 13	10.3
Oct 13	9.6
Nov 13	9.7
Dec 13	10.7
Jan 14	10.1
Feb 14	10.1
Mar 14	10.8
Apr 14	9.9
May 14	9.6
Jun 14	10.2
Jul 14	10.2
Aug 14	10.0
Sep 14	10.0
Oct 14	9.7
Nov 14	10.1
Dec 14	10.2
Jan 15	10.0
Feb 15	10.4
Mar 15	10.6
Apr 15	11.1
May 15	11.0
Jun 15	10.8
Jul 15	11.3
Aug 15	10.7
Sep 15	11.0
Oct 15	10.2
Nov 15	10.3
Dec 15	10.6
Jan 16	11.1
Feb 16	10.9
Mar 16	10.0
Apr 16	10.8
May 16	11.2
Jun 16	11.3
Jul 16	12.9
Aug 16	12.9
Sep 16	12.3
Oct 16	12.9
Nov 16	10.1
Dec 16	13.1
Jan 17	11.5
Feb 17	11.6
Mar 17	10.2
Apr 17	11.1

(*Continued*)

(Continued)

Date	*Multiple*
May 17	11.3
Jun 17	11.2
Jul 17	11.4
Aug 17	11.2
Sep 17	10.7
Oct 17	10.5
Nov 17	10.1
Dec 17	10.6
Jan 18	10.5
Feb 18	10.1
Mar 18	10.3
Apr 18	10.4
May 18	10.1
Jun 18	10.0
Jul 18	10.6
Aug 18	10.2
Sep 18	10.1
Oct 18	10.3
Nov 18	10.1
Dec 18	10.2
Jan 19	10.5
Feb 19	10.2
Mar 19	10.2
Apr 19	10.3
May 19	10.4
Jun 19	10.3
Jul 19	10.4
Aug 19	10.1
Sep 19	10.0
Oct 19	10.6
Nov 19	10.2
Dec 19	10.1
Jan 20	10.3
Feb 20	10.1
Mar 20	10.2
Apr 20	10.5
May 20	10.2
Jun 20	10.2
Jul 20	10.3
Aug 20	10.3
Sep 20	10.2
Oct 20	10.1
Nov 20	10.2
Dec 20	10.1
Jan 21	10.0
Feb 21	10.1
Mar 21	10.2
Apr 21	9.8
May 21	10.0
Jun 21	8.8
Jul 21	9.2

(*Continued*)

(Continued)

Date	*Multiple*
Aug 21	9.1
Sep 21	8.8
Oct 21	7.6
Nov 21	7.5
Dec 21	7.2
Jan 22	6.9
Feb 22	6.1
Mar 22	5.9
Apr 22	5.7
May 22	5.0
Jun 22	5.3
Jul 22	5.0
Aug 22	4.9
Sep 22	5.1
Oct 22	5.1
Nov 22	5.2
Dec 22	5.8
Jan 23	5.3
Feb 23	5.5
Mar 23	5.3
Apr 23	5.6
May 23	5.4
Jun 23	5.3
Jul 23	5.3
Aug 23	5.6
Sep 23	5.4
Oct 23	5.5
Nov 23	5.4
Dec 23	5.3
Jan 24	5.3
Feb 24	5.4
Mar 24	5.2
Apr 24	5.1
May 24	5.2
Jun 24	5.1
Jul 24	5.2
Aug 24	5.0
Sep 24	5.2
Oct 24	5.6
Nov 24	5.6
Dec 24	5.7
Jan 25	5.7
Feb 25	5.6
Mar 25	5.7
Apr 25	5.9
May 25	5.8
Jun 25	5.7
Jul 25	6.0
Aug 25	6.0
Sep 25	6.2
Oct 25	6.2

Key Observations

1 **Stability Period (1993–2008)**: Multiples remained relatively stable between 5.0 and 5.4, with only minor fluctuations corresponding to interest rate movements.
2 **Crisis Period (2008–2009)**: A dramatic increase in multiples from 5.3 to 10.1 as interest rates collapsed from 5% to 0.5% following the banking crisis.
3 **Extended Low Rate Period (2009–2021)**: Multiples of profit remained elevated between 9.6 and 13.1, reflecting the sustained period of ultra-low interest rates.
4 **Return to 'Normal' Rates (2021–2025)**: Profit multiples declined from 10.2 to 5.0 as interest rates rose from 0.1% to 5.25%, a more 'normal' level.

The interesting aspect of profit multiple valuation movements during periods 3 and 4 is that in the former the rapid reduction in interest rates was not anticipated, so the rise in asset values followed the fall in rates. Conversely, in period 4, the interest rate rises were widely anticipated, and so asset values fell in advance of the expected rate rises.

Notable Exceptions

- **October 1994** (3.5 multiple): This business is located in an area with a high proportion of non-English-speaking residents. This reduced the potential pool of buyers.
- **July–December 2016** (three multiples of 12.9 and one of 13.1): One European pharmacy wholesale and retail owner in particular anticipated that the ECB would set negative interest rates in the Eurozone. So that firm instructed its subsidiaries to invest surplus cash in profitable assets, but not in a way that was too concerned with a return on capital. That decision and instruction resulted in the subsidiaries (certainly in the UK) paying premium prices for assets.
- **2020–2021**: The COVID-19 pandemic period did not affect profit multiples. Profits moved due to extra costs in the sector and subsequent payments to cover those costs, but the multiples of profit remained consistent with the model.

This data forms the empirical foundation for the central thesis of this book, which is that in effectively closed markets, asset values move in inverse proportion to interest rate movements, with the relationship becoming more pronounced as rates approach zero.

Appendix B: Official Bank of England Interest Rates

This appendix provides the complete series of official Bank of England interest rates. This corresponds to the period covered by the business transaction data in Appendix A. These rates form the basis for Chart 2 in Chapter 10 and the comparative analysis shown in Charts 3 and 4.

Methodology Note

The interest rates shown are the official Bank of England base rates as published by the Bank of England. During the period covered, the official rate has been known by various names, including 'minimum band 1 dealing rate', 'repo rate', 'minimum lending rate' and 'official bank rate'. The economic function and impact on market conditions remained consistent throughout these changes in name. In May 1997, the Bank of England Monetary Policy Committee began setting the official rate independently of the government. Prior to that, the rate was set by the Chancellor of the Exchequer.

Monthly Interest Rates: May 1993 to October 2025[1]

Date	*Rate*
May 93	5.875
Jun 93	5.875
Jul 93	5.875
Aug 93	5.875
Sep 93	5.875
Oct 93	5.875
Nov 93	5.375
Dec 93	5.375
Jan 94	5.375
Feb 94	5.125
Mar 94	5.125
Apr 94	5.125
May 94	5.125
Jun 94	5.125
Jul 94	5.125
Aug 94	5.125
Sep 94	5.625
Oct 94	5.625
Nov 94	5.625
Dec 94	6.125
Jan 95	6.125
Feb 95	6.625
Mar 95	6.625
Apr 95	6.625
May 95	6.625

(*Continued*)

(Continued)

Date	*Rate*
Jun 95	6.625
Jul 95	6.625
Aug 95	6.625
Sep 95	6.625
Oct 95	6.625
Nov 95	6.625
Dec 95	6.375
Jan 96	6.125
Feb 96	6.125
Mar 96	5.9375
Apr 96	5.9375
May 96	5.9375
Jun 96	5.6875
Jul 96	5.6875
Aug 96	5.6875
Sep 96	5.6875
Oct 96	5.9375
Nov 96	5.9375
Dec 96	5.9375
Jan 97	5.9375
Feb 97	5.9375
Mar 97	5.9375
Apr 97	5.9375
May 97	6.25
Jun 97	6.5
Jul 97	6.75
Aug 97	7.0
Sep 97	7.0
Oct 97	7.0
Nov 97	7.25
Dec 97	7.25
Jan 98	7.25
Feb 98	7.25
Mar 98	7.25
Apr 98	7.25
May 98	7.25
Jun 98	7.5
Jul 98	7.5
Aug 98	7.5
Sep 98	7.5
Oct 98	7.25
Nov 98	6.75
Dec 98	6.25
Jan 99	6.0
Feb 99	5.5
Mar 99	5.5
Apr 99	5.25
May 99	5.25

(*Continued*)

(Continued)

Date	*Rate*
Jun 99	5.0
Jul 99	5.0
Aug 99	5.0
Sep 99	5.25
Oct 99	5.25
Nov 99	5.5
Dec 99	5.5
Jan 00	5.75
Feb 00	6.0
Mar 00	6.0
Apr 00	6.0
May 00	6.0
Jun 00	6.0
Jul 00	6.0
Aug 00	6.0
Sep 00	6.0
Oct 00	6.0
Nov 00	6.0
Dec 00	6.0
Jan 01	6.0
Feb 01	5.75
Mar 01	5.75
Apr 01	5.5
May 01	5.25
Jun 01	5.25
Jul 01	5.25
Aug 01	5.0
Sep 01	4.75
Oct 01	4.5
Nov 01	4.0
Dec 01	4.0
Jan 02	4.0
Feb 02	4.0
Mar 02	4.0
Apr 02	4.0
May 02	4.0
Jun 02	4.0
Jul 02	4.0
Aug 02	4.0
Sep 02	4.0
Oct 02	4.0
Nov 02	4.0
Dec 02	4.0
Jan 03	4.0
Feb 03	3.75
Mar 03	3.75
Apr 03	3.75
May 03	3.75

(*Continued*)

(Continued)

Date	*Rate*
Jun 03	3.75
Jul 03	3.5
Aug 03	3.5
Sep 03	3.5
Oct 03	3.5
Nov 03	3.75
Dec 03	3.75
Jan 04	3.75
Feb 04	4.0
Mar 04	4.0
Apr 04	4.0
May 04	4.25
Jun 04	4.5
Jul 04	4.5
Aug 04	4.75
Sep 04	4.75
Oct 04	4.75
Nov 04	4.75
Dec 04	4.75
Jan 05	4.75
Feb 05	4.75
Mar 05	4.75
Apr 05	4.75
May 05	4.75
Jun 05	4.75
Jul 05	4.75
Aug 05	4.5
Sep 05	4.5
Oct 05	4.5
Nov 05	4.5
Dec 05	4.5
Jan 06	4.5
Feb 06	4.5
Mar 06	4.5
Apr 06	4.5
May 06	4.5
Jun 06	4.5
Jul 06	4.5
Aug 06	4.75
Sep 06	4.75
Oct 06	4.75
Nov 06	5.0
Dec 06	5.0
Jan 07	5.25
Feb 07	5.25
Mar 07	5.25
Apr 07	5.25
May 07	5.5

(*Continued*)

(Continued)

Date	*Rate*
Jun 07	5.5
Jul 07	5.75
Aug 07	5.75
Sep 07	5.75
Oct 07	5.75
Nov 07	5.75
Dec 07	5.5
Jan 08	5.5
Feb 08	5.25
Mar 08	5.25
Apr 08	5.0
May 08	5.0
Jun 08	5.0
Jul 08	5.0
Aug 08	5.0
Sep 08	5.0
Oct 08	4.5
Nov 08	3.0
Dec 08	2.0
Jan 09	1.5
Feb 09	1.0
Mar 09	0.5
Apr 09	0.5
May 09	0.5
Jun 09	0.5
Jul 09	0.5
Aug 09	0.5
Sep 09	0.5
Oct 09	0.5
Nov 09	0.5
Dec 09	0.5
Jan 10	0.5
Feb 10	0.5
Mar 10	0.5
Apr 10	0.5
May 10	0.5
Jun 10	0.5
Jul 10	0.5
Aug 10	0.5
Sep 10	0.5
Oct 10	0.5
Nov 10	0.5
Dec 10	0.5
Jan 11	0.5
Feb 11	0.5
Mar 11	0.5
Apr 11	0.5
May 11	0.5

(*Continued*)

(Continued)

Date	*Rate*
Jun 11	0.5
Jul 11	0.5
Aug 11	0.5
Sep 11	0.5
Oct 11	0.5
Nov 11	0.5
Dec 11	0.5
Jan 12	0.5
Feb 12	0.5
Mar 12	0.5
Apr 12	0.5
May 12	0.5
Jun 12	0.5
Jul 12	0.5
Aug 12	0.5
Sep 12	0.5
Oct 12	0.5
Nov 12	0.5
Dec 12	0.5
Jan 13	0.5
Feb 13	0.5
Mar 13	0.5
Apr 13	0.5
May 13	0.5
Jun 13	0.5
Jul 13	0.5
Aug 13	0.5
Sep 13	0.5
Oct 13	0.5
Nov 13	0.5
Dec 13	0.5
Jan 14	0.5
Feb 14	0.5
Mar 14	0.5
Apr 14	0.5
May 14	0.5
Jun 14	0.5
Jul 14	0.5
Aug 14	0.5
Sep 14	0.5
Oct 14	0.5
Nov 14	0.5
Dec 14	0.5
Jan 15	0.5
Feb 15	0.5
Mar 15	0.5
Apr 15	0.5
May 15	0.5

(*Continued*)

(Continued)

Date	*Rate*
Jun 15	0.5
Jul 15	0.5
Aug 15	0.5
Sep 15	0.5
Oct 15	0.5
Nov 15	0.5
Dec 15	0.5
Jan 16	0.5
Feb 16	0.5
Mar 16	0.5
Apr 16	0.5
May 16	0.5
Jun 16	0.5
Jul 16	0.5
Aug 16	0.25
Sep 16	0.25
Oct 16	0.25
Nov 16	0.25
Dec 16	0.25
Jan 17	0.25
Feb 17	0.25
Mar 17	0.25
Apr 17	0.25
May 17	0.25
Jun 17	0.25
Jul 17	0.25
Aug 17	0.25
Sep 17	0.25
Oct 17	0.25
Nov 17	0.5
Dec 17	0.5
Jan 18	0.5
Feb 18	0.5
Mar 18	0.5
Apr 18	0.5
May 18	0.5
Jun 18	0.5
Jul 18	0.5
Aug 18	0.75
Sep 18	0.75
Oct 18	0.75
Nov 18	0.75
Dec 18	0.75
Jan 19	0.75
Feb 19	0.75
Mar 19	0.75
Apr 19	0.75
May 19	0.75

(*Continued*)

(Continued)

Date	*Rate*
Jun 19	0.75
Jul 19	0.75
Aug 19	0.75
Sep 19	0.75
Oct 19	0.75
Nov 19	0.75
Dec 19	0.75
Jan 20	0.75
Feb 20	0.75
Mar 20	0.1
Apr 20	0.1
May 20	0.1
Jun 20	0.1
Jul 20	0.1
Aug 20	0.1
Sep 20	0.1
Oct 20	0.1
Nov 20	0.1
Dec 20	0.1
Jan 21	0.1
Feb 21	0.1
Mar 21	0.1
Apr 21	0.1
May 21	0.1
Jun 21	0.1
Jul 21	0.1
Aug 21	0.1
Sep 21	0.1
Oct 21	0.1
Nov 21	0.1
Dec 21	0.25
Jan 22	0.25
Feb 22	0.5
Mar 22	0.75
Apr 22	0.75
May 22	1.0
Jun 22	1.25
Jul 22	1.25
Aug 22	1.75
Sep 22	2.25
Oct 22	2.25
Nov 22	3.0
Dec 22	3.5
Jan 23	3.5
Feb 23	4.0
Mar 23	4.25
Apr 23	4.25
May 23	4.5

(Continued)

(Continued)

Date	*Rate*
Jun 23	5.0
Jul 23	5.0
Aug 23	5.25
Sep 23	5.25
Oct 23	5.25
Nov 23	5.25
Dec 23	5.25
Jan 24	5.25
Feb 24	5.25
Mar 24	5.25
Apr 24	5.25
May 24	5.25
Jun 24	5.25
Jul 24	5.25
Aug 24	5.0
Sep 24	5.0
Oct 24	5.0
Nov 24	4.75
Dec 24	4.75
Jan 25	4.75
Feb 25	4.5
Mar 25	4.5
Apr 25	4.5
May 25	4.25
Jun 25	4.25
Jul 25	4.25
Aug 25	4.25
Sep 25	4.0
Oct 25	4.0

Key Interest Rate Periods

1. **Normal Rate Environment (1993–2008)**
   Interest rates fluctuated between 3.5% and 7.5%, following traditional monetary policy cycles responding to economic conditions, inflation targets and exchange rate considerations.
2. **Financial Crisis Response (2008–2009)**
   Dramatic reduction from 5% in September 2008 to 0.5% by March 2009, representing the most aggressive monetary policy easing in Bank of England history at that time.
3. **Extended Ultra Low Rate Period (2009–2021)**
   Rates remained at 0.5% for some years. There was an emergency cut in rates to 0.25% immediately after the Brexit referendum result was announced in order to create immediate market stability. While rates rose slightly after that stability was recognised, there was a further cut to

0.1% at the start of the COVID-19 pandemic, again to achieve market stability. This was the lowest rate in the Bank's 330-year history.

4 **Normalisation Period (2021–2025)**
Gradual increase from 0.1% to 5.0%, reflecting post-pandemic economic recovery, inflation concerns, and return to more traditional monetary policy frameworks.

Relationship to Asset Values

This interest rate data, when compared with the business valuation multiples in Appendix A, reveals the remarkable inverse correlation that forms the central finding of this book. The periods of most dramatic change provide the clearest evidence:

- **2008–2009**: As rates fell from 5% to 0.5%, valuation multiples rose from 5.1 to 10.1.
- **2021–2022**: As rates rose from 0.1% to 3.5%, valuation multiples fell from 10.2 to 5.0.

This relationship demonstrates how, in effectively closed markets such as the UK pharmaceutical retail sector, interest rates become the primary determinant of asset values, with the normal market mechanisms of supply and demand playing a secondary role due to regulatory barriers to entry.[2]

Appendix C: Implications for Policymakers, Businesses and Economic Theory

The research presented in this book demonstrates a fundamental relationship between market structure and asset pricing that challenges conventional assumptions about how business values are determined.

Through detailed analysis of 390 transactions over 32 years in the UK retail pharmacy sector, I have established that asset values in markets closed by regulatory barriers respond primarily to interest rate changes rather than competitive forces. Looking at the four graphs in Chapter 10 above (particularly Chart 10.4), we can see graphically the absolute correlation of asset values to interest rates.

This finding has implications that extend far beyond the UK retail pharmacy sector to broader questions about asset pricing, market efficiency, regulatory policy and investment strategy. When artificial scarcity created by regulatory barriers limits competitive forces, the normal mechanisms that drive asset values in open markets are fundamentally altered. Understanding these alterations provides insights relevant to numerous regulated industries and policy contexts.

But it also proves and extends the findings of Gyourko (2009) and Gyourko & Molloy (2015) because we have been able to look at a market where there are no other external factors affecting asset values.

The central conclusion of this research is that market structure matters for asset pricing in ways that are not adequately recognised in conventional financial theory. The assumption that markets are competitive and that asset values reflect fundamental business performance may not hold when regulatory barriers create artificial scarcity in the market. In such circumstances, financial variables such as interest rates become more important than operational factors in determining business values.

This conclusion has practical implications for anyone involved in valuing, buying or selling businesses in regulated industries. It suggests that different analytical approaches may be needed for closed markets than for competitive ones and that macroeconomic factors may be more important in regulated industries than conventional analysis assumes.

But it also spills over (per Gyourko) into non-regulated asset valuations. Although the link between asset values and interest rates is definitively proved by this research because it occurs in a closed market, it does not invalidate that link in open markets. It is merely more difficult to prove in those open markets due to the other factors that bear upon asset prices there, as well as not being such an absolute, robust and strong link.

What This Means for Economic Theory

The findings of this research contribute to several streams of economic theory, particularly those concerning market structure, asset pricing and the effects of regulation on economic behaviour and the link between those three elements. The demonstration of systematic relationships between macroeconomic variables and asset prices in closed markets provides evidence for theoretical propositions that have been difficult to test empirically in open markets.

Market Structure Theory

The research provides empirical validation for theoretical arguments about the importance of market structure in determining economic outcomes. The clear demonstration that asset pricing mechanisms differ fundamentally between open and closed markets supports theoretical work on the effects of barriers to entry on market behaviour.[3]

The findings suggest that market structure effects may be more pervasive and systematic than previously recognised. If similar relationships exist in other regulated industries, the implications for understanding economic behaviour in modern economies could be substantial, given the prevalence of regulatory barriers across many sectors, not only in the United Kingdom but worldwide.

The research also demonstrates how multiple regulatory mechanisms can combine to create market closure that is more comprehensive than any individual barrier would achieve. This finding contributes to understanding of how regulatory frameworks interact to produce economic effects that may not be apparent from examination of individual regulations. We have seen market closure can come about both through market mechanisms such as integration and disintegration and by the imposition of regulatory control.

However, it cannot be emphasised enough that the effect of interest rates on asset values is not necessarily limited to closed markets. This work merely proves the link between asset values and interest rates by using a closed market example so that the link can be empirically proved. While open markets are much more difficult in proving the link due to other external factors, it does not mean the link does not exist at all (as shown by Gyourko).

Asset Pricing Theory

Traditional asset pricing theory focuses primarily on systematic risk factors and fundamental business performance as drivers of asset values. The UK retail pharmacy sector evidence studied in this book suggests that in closed markets, these factors may be less important than financial variables that reflect the cost of capital.[4]

This finding does not invalidate asset pricing theory but suggests that its application may need modification in closed market conditions. The mechanisms identified in finance theory still operate, but their relative importance changes when competitive forces are constrained by regulatory barriers.

The research demonstrates that duration-like characteristics typically associated with fixed income securities can also apply to business assets when cash flows are protected from competitive erosion. This suggests potential applications of fixed income analytical techniques to business valuation in regulated industries.

Regulatory Economics

The systematic effects of regulatory barriers on asset pricing provide new insights into the economic consequences of regulation. Previous research has focused primarily on static efficiency effects and direct compliance costs, while the dynamic effects on asset markets have received less attention.

The demonstration that regulatory barriers can create predictable relationships between macroeconomic variables and asset prices suggests that regulation may have broader economic effects than previously recognised. These effects may contribute to asset price volatility and create systemic risks that extend beyond directly regulated sectors.[5]

The findings also suggest that the economic evaluation of regulatory proposals should include analysis of their potential effects on asset markets and financial stability, in addition to traditional analysis of efficiency and compliance effects.

Financial Market Integration

The research provides evidence for how regulatory segmentation can prevent financial market integration that would normally arbitrage away systematic pricing relationships. The barriers that create artificial scarcity also prevent the arbitrage activity that would eliminate predictable asset pricing patterns.

This finding contributes to understanding how market segmentation affects financial market efficiency and the transmission of macroeconomic shocks through different sectors of the economy. Regulated industries may respond differently to macroeconomic changes than competitive sectors.[6]

The implications extend to understanding of monetary policy transmission mechanisms, suggesting that regulatory barriers may affect how interest rate changes influence different sectors of the economy.

Practical Applications for Investors and Policymakers

The insights developed through this research have immediate practical applications for investors, policymakers and business practitioners who operate in or regulate closed markets. Understanding how market closure affects asset pricing can inform better decision-making across multiple contexts.

Investment Strategy Applications

For investors operating in regulated industries, the demonstrated relationship between interest rates and asset values provides a framework for timing investment decisions and managing portfolio risk. The predictability of asset value responses to interest rate changes enables more sophisticated investment strategies than would be possible in competitive markets.[7]

Investment timing strategies can be developed based on interest rate forecasts, while portfolio construction can account for the different risk/return characteristics of assets in closed versus competitive markets. The duration-like characteristics of closed market assets may provide diversification benefits for investment portfolios.

However, the same barriers that create predictable relationships also limit the scale at which investment strategies can be implemented. Entry barriers that make asset values predictable also prevent large-scale arbitrage that could capture these predictable returns.

Business Valuation Practice

Professional business valuers working in regulated industries need to account for the systematic effects of market closure on asset pricing. Traditional valuation approaches that assume competitive market conditions may systematically underestimate or overestimate values in closed markets.

The research provides a framework for adjusting valuation methods to account for closed market conditions, including modification of discount rates, cash flow projections and risk assessments. This framework can improve valuation accuracy and reduce disputes in business transactions.[8]

Understanding the interest rate relationship also enables more sophisticated transaction timing advice for buyers and sellers in regulated industries. Knowledge of how asset values respond to interest rate changes can inform decisions about when to enter markets or complete transactions.

Regulatory Policy Development

For policymakers, the research demonstrates that regulatory decisions about market structure have significant effects on asset pricing and financial market behaviour. These effects should be considered in the design and evaluation of regulatory frameworks, alongside traditional considerations of market efficiency and consumer protection.

The findings suggest that regulatory barriers may contribute to asset price volatility and create systemic risks through their effects on the relationship between macroeconomic variables and asset values. Policymakers should consider these financial stability implications when designing regulatory frameworks.[9]

The research also provides a framework for evaluating the economic costs and benefits of regulatory barriers. The systematic effects on asset pricing represent economic costs that should be weighed against the benefits of regulation in terms of market stability, consumer protection, or other policy objectives.

Competition Policy Applications

Competition authorities need to consider not only the direct effects of market concentration and barriers to entry but also their indirect effects on asset pricing and financial market behaviour. Market closure may create systemic risks that extend beyond the directly affected sectors.

The research demonstrates how multiple regulatory mechanisms can combine to create market closure that is more comprehensive than any individual barrier would achieve. This finding suggests that competition analysis should examine the cumulative effects of regulatory frameworks rather than individual barriers in isolation.[10]

Understanding how market closure affects asset pricing may also inform competition policy decisions about when intervention is necessary and what forms of intervention are likely to be most effective in restoring competitive market conditions.

The Broader Significance of Closed Market Dynamics

The implications of this research extend beyond immediate applications to broader questions about economic organisation and the effects of regulatory frameworks on market behaviour. The findings contribute to understanding of how modern economies function when significant sectors operate under regulatory constraints that limit competitive forces.

Prevalence of Closed Markets

Analysis of the UK economy reveals that regulated industries subject to entry barriers are more prevalent than initially appear. Professional services, licensed premises, financial services and numerous other sectors operate under regulatory frameworks, creating varying degrees of market closure.[11]

If the principles demonstrated in the pharmaceutical sector apply to other closed markets, the implications for understanding asset pricing across the broader economy could be substantial. The systematic effects of regulatory barriers on asset prices may contribute to macroeconomic relationships that are not adequately captured in conventional economic models.

The prevalence of closed markets also suggests that the assumptions underlying much economic theory about competitive market conditions may not reflect the reality of how significant portions of modern economies actually operate.

Systemic Risk Considerations

The systematic relationship between interest rates and asset values in closed markets may contribute to systemic risks in the financial system. If multiple regulated industries exhibit similar relationships, interest rate changes could have amplified effects on asset values across substantial portions of the economy.

These amplified effects could contribute to financial instability during periods of significant interest rate changes, particularly if financial institutions have concentrated exposure to regulated industries. Understanding these risks requires analysis of the effects of market closure across multiple sectors.[12]

The systemic implications suggest that financial stability analysis should consider not only direct exposures to interest rate risk but also indirect exposures through assets in closed markets that may exhibit enhanced interest rate sensitivity.

Monetary Policy Transmission

The findings have implications for understanding how monetary policy affects different sectors of the economy. If regulated industries respond differently to interest rate changes than competitive sectors, this may affect the overall transmission mechanism of monetary policy.

The enhanced sensitivity of asset values to interest rate changes in closed markets may create transmission channels that operate more directly and predictably than in competitive markets. This could affect both the timing and magnitude of monetary policy effects on economic activity.[13]

Understanding these differential transmission effects may inform monetary policy decisions about the appropriate level and timing of interest rate changes needed to achieve desired economic effects.

Financial Market Development

The research provides insights into how regulatory frameworks affect financial market development and the pricing of different types of assets. Markets that develop in closed conditions may exhibit different characteristics than those in open markets.

The findings suggest that financial markets may be more segmented than conventional theory assumes, with different sectors exhibiting different relationships between systematic factors and asset prices. This segmentation may affect portfolio construction, risk management and investment strategy across multiple asset classes.[14]

Future Research Directions

The findings of this research open several avenues for future investigation that could extend and refine our understanding of asset pricing in closed markets. These research directions could contribute to both theoretical development and practical applications across multiple disciplines.

Extension to Other Regulated Industries

The most immediate research opportunity involves testing whether similar relationships exist in other regulated industries that exhibit market closure characteristics. Sectors including taxi services, broadcasting, medical practices and licensed premises all exhibit regulatory barriers that may create similar asset pricing dynamics.

Systematic analysis across multiple regulated industries could establish whether the principles demonstrated in the pharmaceutical sector represent general characteristics of closed markets or industry-specific phenomena. Such analysis could also identify the specific regulatory characteristics that are most important in creating systematic asset pricing relationships.[15]

Cross-industry analysis could also reveal whether the magnitude and persistence of interest rate relationships vary with different types of regulatory barriers, enabling more precise prediction of where similar effects might be expected.

International Comparative Analysis

Examination of pharmaceutical markets in other countries with different regulatory frameworks could test whether the observed relationships depend on specific characteristics of UK regulation or represent more general effects of market closure. Countries with different approaches to pharmacy regulation provide natural experiments in how regulatory design affects asset pricing.

International comparison could also examine whether the interest rate relationship varies with different macroeconomic environments, monetary policy regimes or financial market structures. Such analysis could contribute to understanding of how institutional factors affect the transmission of macroeconomic effects through regulated industries.[16]

Dynamic Analysis of Market Opening and Closure

Longitudinal studies of markets that transition between competitive and closed conditions may provide insights into the mechanisms driving the interest rate relationship. Deregulation events provide natural experiments in how asset pricing changes when markets transition from closed to open conditions.

Similarly, analysis of markets that become more regulated over time could examine how increasing closure affects asset pricing relationships. Such dynamic analysis could provide stronger evidence for causal relationships and better understanding of the mechanisms involved.[17]

Financial Market Integration Studies

Research into how closed market assets interact with broader financial markets could examine whether the relationships identified in this study affect portfolio risk, diversification benefits and overall financial market stability.

Analysis of how closed market asset prices correlate with other asset classes could reveal whether market closure creates systematic risks that extend beyond individual sectors. Such research could inform both investment strategy and financial stability policy.[18]

Regulatory Design Optimisation

Future research could examine how regulatory frameworks could be designed to achieve policy objectives while minimising unintended effects on asset pricing and financial market behaviour. This could contribute to better regulatory design that balances market efficiency with other policy goals.

Analysis of different regulatory approaches across industries and countries could identify best practices for achieving regulatory objectives while preserving competitive market conditions where possible or managing the effects of necessary market closure where competition is not feasible.

Practical Recommendations

Based on the findings of this research, several practical recommendations emerge for different stakeholders involved in or affected by closed market conditions.

For Investors

Investors operating in regulated industries should recognise that conventional asset pricing models may not adequately capture the dynamics of closed markets. Investment strategies should account for the enhanced sensitivity of asset values to interest rate changes and the reduced importance of traditional competitive factors.[19]

Portfolio construction in regulated industries should consider the duration-like characteristics of closed market assets and their potential correlation with interest rate cycles. Risk management approaches should account for regulatory risks alongside traditional business risks.

Due diligence for investments in regulated industries should include analysis of the regulatory barriers that create market closure and assessment of their sustainability over the investment horizon. Understanding the mechanisms that create artificial scarcity is crucial for evaluating investment risks and returns.

For Business Owners and Managers

Business owners in regulated industries should recognise that their business values are more sensitive to macroeconomic conditions than might be typical in competitive markets. Business strategy should account for this sensitivity in planning major decisions about expansion, acquisition or disposal.

Financial management in closed markets should consider the effects of leverage and financial structure on sensitivity to interest rate changes. The predictable relationship between rates and values may inform optimal capital structure decisions and financing strategies.[20]

Strategic planning should account for the regulatory foundations that create market closure and develop contingency plans for potential changes in regulatory frameworks that could affect market structure and asset values.

For Policymakers

Regulatory authorities should consider the effects of market structure decisions on asset pricing and financial stability alongside traditional considerations of market efficiency and consumer protection. The systematic effects demonstrated in this research represent economic costs that should be weighed against regulatory benefits.

Competition policy should examine not only direct effects of market concentration but also indirect effects through asset pricing mechanisms. The cumulative effects of multiple regulatory barriers may create more comprehensive market closure than intended by individual regulations.[21]

Financial stability authorities should consider the potential for systematic relationships between macroeconomic variables and asset prices in regulated industries to contribute to financial instability during periods of significant interest rate changes.

For Professional Advisers

Business valuers, corporate finance advisers and other professionals working in regulated industries should adapt their methodologies to account for the distinctive characteristics of closed markets. Traditional approaches that assume competitive conditions may provide misleading results.

The development of specialised expertise in closed market valuation could improve service quality and reduce disputes in business transactions. Understanding the systematic relationships demonstrated in this research could enhance the accuracy and relevance of professional advice.[22]

Professional education and training programmes should include coverage of closed market dynamics and their implications for business analysis, ensuring that practitioners understand how regulatory barriers affect the application of standard analytical techniques.

Final Conclusions

This research demonstrates that the relationship between interest rates and asset values in closed markets is both stronger and more systematic than conventional economic theory predicts. The UK pharmaceutical sector provides compelling evidence that when regulatory barriers create artificial scarcity and limit competitive forces, asset values respond primarily to changes in the cost of capital rather than to operational or competitive factors.

Theoretical Contributions

The research contributes to economic theory by providing empirical evidence for the importance of market structure in asset pricing, demonstrating how regulatory barriers can create systematic relationships between macroeconomic variables and business values, and showing how financial theory mechanisms operate with unusual clarity in closed market conditions.

These contributions suggest that economic models may need to account more explicitly for the effects of regulatory barriers on market behaviour and that asset pricing theory may require modification when applied to regulated industries where competitive assumptions do not hold.

Practical Implications

The practical implications encompass improved approaches to business valuation in regulated industries, enhanced investment strategies that account for closed market dynamics and better regulatory policy that considers unintended effects on asset pricing and financial stability.

For the pharmaceutical industry specifically, the findings provide a framework for understanding how regulatory changes, interest rate cycles and market structure evolution affect business values and investment returns. This understanding can inform better decision-making by all market participants.

Broader Significance

The broader significance of this research lies in its demonstration that regulatory frameworks have systematic effects on economic behaviour that extend beyond their intended scope. Market closure created for policy reasons generates unintended consequences for asset pricing and financial market behaviour that may contribute to systemic risks.

Understanding these systematic effects is crucial for designing effective regulatory frameworks that achieve policy objectives while minimising unintended economic costs. The research provides tools for analysing these effects and frameworks for incorporating them into policy decisions.

Future Development

The findings presented in this book represent the foundation for a research programme that could extend to multiple regulated industries and contribute to better understanding of how modern economies function when significant sectors operate under regulatory constraints.

The methodological approaches developed here could be applied to other sectors to test how general the findings are and develop a more comprehensive understanding of closed market dynamics. But it should be pointed out that comparisons would only be valid where the market examined is similarly closed to new entrants. Such research could contribute to both theoretical development and practical applications across multiple policy and business contexts.[23]

The insurance model of vertical integration identified in this research merits separate development as a theoretical framework for understanding how firms adapt to regulatory constraints while pursuing competitive advantages. This model could provide insights applicable to numerous industries and regulatory contexts.

Methodological Contributions

The research demonstrates the value of comprehensive longitudinal analysis in testing economic relationships, showing how extensive transaction datasets can provide insights not available through shorter-term or smaller-scale studies. The methodological approaches developed here could be applied to other regulated industries to test how or if the findings can be applied more generally.[24]

The integration of theoretical analysis with empirical investigation provides a model for research that bridges academic theory and practical application. This approach enables findings that are both theoretically grounded and practically relevant.

As with all research, other researchers may find slightly different results.

Obviously, the interest rate side of the equation (Bank of England base lending rate for the periods of the research and comparisons) is an established fact.

In terms of the price multiples of the asset sales, how robust can they be taken as?

The random one trade per month for the 32-year study period is truly random. Having chosen a random business transaction that month, others were viewed to check that the random set of accounts was not rogue. The comparisons bore up the original data chosen, by being only one or two decimal points either side of the original. A few were outliers. These are highlighted and explained in the analysis.

Having checked for outliers, it is felt that were another researcher to carry out similar work, the resulting interest rate to asset graphs would be remarkably similar to those demonstrated in this book, showing exactly the same correlation with interest rates. While the sale price multiple line of the graph would not be absolutely identical, the movements would track the same pattern.

Appendix D: Notes on Confidential Sources

This research draws extensively on confidential commercial information obtained through 30 years of professional practice and industry relationships in the UK pharmaceutical sector. The author's consultancy work provided unique access to internal business information, transaction details and strategic documentation not available through public sources.

While specific attribution of confidential sources is limited by professional obligations and commercial sensitivities, all material claims have been cross-referenced and validated through multiple sources. The combination of confidential industry access with rigorous academic methodology provides a comprehensive empirical foundation unavailable through either approach alone.

The use of primary source material reflects the necessity of understanding actual market behaviour and commercial relationships rather than relying solely on published sources that may not capture the complexity of industry dynamics and strategic decision-making.

The primary source material could be made available on a confidential basis to researchers wishing to validate the findings of this book, in line with confidentiality agreements entered into in order to obtain that material.

Notes

1 The source of the data was the Bank of England official bank rate history data chart (www.bankofengland.co.uk).
2 Bank of England Statistical Interactive Database, Official Bank Rate series (IUDBEDR) and related monetary statistics, accessed throughout the research period.
3 The empirical validation of market structure theory builds on foundational work by Bain, J.S. (1956), Barriers to New Competition, Harvard University Press, and subsequent developments in industrial organisation economics.
4 Asset pricing theory implications relate to extensions of the Capital Asset Pricing Model and Arbitrage Pricing Theory to account for market structure effects not considered in the original formulations.
5 Regulatory economics implications build on work by Stigler, G.J. (1971), The Theory of Economic Regulation, Bell Journal of Economics, Vol. 2, pp. 3–21, and subsequent literature on regulatory capture and unintended consequences.
6 Financial market integration analysis relates to literature on market segmentation and its effects on asset pricing, including work on international market integration and regulatory barriers to arbitrage.
7 Investment strategy applications draw on portfolio theory and asset allocation literature, adapted to account for the distinctive characteristics of closed market assets.
8 Professional valuation practice recommendations build on established business valuation literature while adapting to closed market conditions identified in this research.
9 Financial stability implications relate to literature on systemic risk and the transmission of macroeconomic shocks through different sectors of the economy.
10 Competition policy implications build on industrial organisation literature and empirical studies of regulatory barriers and market concentration effects.
11 Analysis of closed market prevalence based on examination of regulatory frameworks across multiple UK industries and comparison with international experience.
12 Systemic risk analysis adapted from financial stability literature and applied to the specific characteristics of regulated industry asset pricing.
13 Monetary policy transmission analysis builds on central banking literature and empirical studies of interest rate effects across different economic sectors.
14 Financial market development implications relate to literature on market microstructure and the effects of regulatory frameworks on price discovery mechanisms.

15 Cross-industry research directions based on preliminary analysis of regulatory characteristics across multiple UK industries with potential closed market characteristics.
16 International comparative analysis opportunities identified through examination of pharmaceutical regulatory frameworks in developed economies with available transaction data.
17 Dynamic analysis research directions based on historical examples of regulatory change and market structure transitions in the United Kingdom and other developed economies.
18 Financial market integration research directions relate to portfolio theory and systemic risk literature applied to regulated industry characteristics.
19 Investor recommendation development based on application of portfolio theory and investment strategy literature to closed market asset characteristics.
20 Business owner recommendations based on corporate finance literature adapted to account for closed market conditions and enhanced interest rate sensitivity.
21 Policymaker recommendations based on regulatory economics literature and empirical evidence from this research on unintended consequences of market closure.
22 Professional adviser recommendations based on business valuation literature and professional practice standards adapted for closed market conditions.
23 Future research development based on assessment of research opportunities across multiple regulated industries and policy contexts where similar market closure conditions may exist.
24 Methodological contributions relate to empirical research design literature and longitudinal study methodology adapted for private market transaction analysis.

Bibliography

Anderton, A., 1991. *Economics*. Causeway Press.

Arrow, K. J., 1969. *The Organisation of Market Activity. Issues Pertinent to the Choice of Market Versus Nonmarket Allocation in the Analysis and Evaluation of Public Expenditures: The PPB System* (Vol. 1). Joint Economic Committee, Washington, D.C.

Auerbach, P., 1990. *Vertical Integration. Planning and the Market*. The APEX Centre, Kingston University.

Austen, J., 1811. *Sense and Sensibility*. Penguin Classics, 2003, Reprint, London.

Austen, J., 1813. *Pride and Prejudice*. In Kinsley, J. (ed). Oxford World's Classics, Oxford University Press, 2004.

Austen, J., 1818. *Persuasion*. In Harding, D. W. (ed). Penguin Classics, 1998.

Bain, J. S., 1956. *Barriers to New Competition*. Harvard University Press, Cambridge, MA.

Bernanke, B. S., & Gertler, M., 1995. *Inside the Black Box: The Credit Channel of Monetary Policy Transmission*. Journal of Economic Perspectives, 9 (4), 27–48.

Blair, R. D., & Kaserman, D. L., 1983. *Law and Economics of Vertical Integration and Control*. Academic Press Inc.

Bodie, Z., Kane, A., & Marcus, A. J., 2021. *Investments* (12th Edition). McGraw Hill.

Bordo, M. D., & Eichengreen, B., 1993. *A Retrospective on the Bretton Woods System: Lessons for International Monetary Reform*. University of Chicago Press.

Borio, C., & Lowe, P., 2002. Asset Prices, Financial and Monetary Stability: Exploring the Nexus. BIS Working Papers No. 114.

Brealey, R. A., Myers, S. C., & Allen, F., 2020. *Principles of Corporate Finance* (13th Edition). McGraw-Hill.

Campbell, J. Y., & Shiller, R. J., 1988. *Stock Prices, Earnings, and Expected Dividends*. Journal of Finance, 43 (3), 661–676.

Campbell, J. Y., & Shiller, R. J., 1988. *The Dividend-Price Ratio and Expectations of Future Dividends and Discount Factors*. The Review of Financial Studies, 1 (3), 195–228.

Chandler, A. D., 1977. *The Visible Hand*. Belknap Press of Harvard University.

Chandler, A. D., 1990. *Scale and Scope*. Belknap Press of Harvard University.

Chen, K., Chen, X., & Lee, C., 2019. *Interest Rate Liberalization and Asset Prices: Evidence from China*. Journal of Financial Economics, 132 (1), 128–152.

Cipolla, C. M., 1956. *Money, Prices, and Civilization in the Mediterranean World, Fifth to Seventeenth Century*. Princeton University Press.

Coase, R., 1937. The Nature of the Firm. *Economics* (Vol. 4). Reprinted in Williamson, O. E. & Winter, S. G. (eds), 1991. The Nature of the Firm: Origins. Evolution and Development. Oxford University Press.

Cochrane, J. H., 2005. *Asset Pricing* (Revised Edition). Princeton University Press.

Culbertson, J. M., 1957. *The Term Structure of Interest Rates*. Quarterly Journal of Economics, 71 (4), 485–517.

Dnes, A. W., 1992. *Franchising: A Case Study Approach*. Avebury Ashgate Publishing Ltd.

Eichengreen, B., 2008. *Globalizing Capital: A History of the International Monetary System* (2nd Edition). Princeton University Press.

Estrella, A., & Mishkin, F. S., 1996. *The Yield Curve as a Predictor of U.* Recessions. Current Issues in Economics and Finance, 2 (7), 1–6.

Fama, E. F., & French, K. R., 1993. *Common Risk Factors in the Returns on Stocks and Bonds*. Journal of Financial Economics, 33 (1), 3–56.

Fama, E. F., & French, K. R., 2004. *The Capital Asset Pricing Model: Theory and Evidence*. Journal of Economic Perspectives, 18 (3), 25–46.

Fama, E. F., & MacBeth, J. D., 1973. *Risk, Return, and Equilibrium: Empirical Tests*. Journal of Political Economy, 81 (3), 607–636.

Ferguson, N., 2008. *The Ascent of Money: A Financial History of the World*. Penguin.

Fisher, I., 1930. *The Theory of Interest*. Macmillan.

Flynn, D. O., & Giráldez, A., 1995. *Born with a 'Silver Spoon': The Origin of World Trade in 1571*. Journal of World History, 6 (2), 201–221.

Friedman, M., 1956. The Quantity Theory of Money—A Restatement. In Friedman, M. (ed), *Studies in the Quantity Theory of Money* (pp. 3–21). University of Chicago Press.

Friedman, M., 1963. *Inflation: Causes and Consequences*. Asia Publishing House.

Friedman, M., 1968. *The Role of Monetary Policy*. American Economic Review, 58 (1), 1–17.

Glaser, B. G., 1978. *Theoretical Sensitivity: Advances in the Methodology of Grounded Theory*. Sociology Press.

Green, F., & Sutcliffe, B., 1987. *The Profit System*. Penguin.

Gujarati, D. N., & Porter, D. C., 2009. *Basic Econometrics* (5th Edition). McGraw Hill, New York.

Gyourko, J., 2009. *Housing Supply*. Annual Review of Economics, 1, 295–318.

Gyourko, J., & Molloy, R., 2015. *Regulation and Housing Supply*. Annual Review of Economics, 7 (1), 827–844.

Hamilton, E. J., 1934. *American Treasure and the Price Revolution in Spain, 1501–1650*. Harvard University Press.

Hansen, B. E., 2001. *The New Econometrics of Structural Change*. Journal of Economic Perspectives, 15, 117–128.

Hansen, L. P., 1982. *Large Sample Properties of Generalized Method of Moments Estimators*. Econometrica, 50 (4), 1029–1054.

Hansen, L. P., & Singleton, K. J., 1982. *Generalized Instrumental Variables Estimation of Nonlinear Rational Expectations Models*. Econometrica, 50 (5), 1269–1286.

Hart, O. D., 1989. Incomplete Contracts and the Theory of the Firm. Reprinted in Williamson, O. E. & Winter, S. G. (eds), 1991. *The Nature of the Firm: Origins. Evolution and Development*. Oxford University Press.

Hayek, F. A., 1941. *The Pure Theory of Capital*. Macmillan.

Hayek, F. A., 1945. *The Use of Knowledge in Society*. The American Economic Review, 35 (4), 519–530.

Hayek, F. A., 1974. The Pretence of Knowledge. Nobel Memorial Lecture, December 11, 1974.

Hayek, F. A., 1978. *New Studies in Philosophy, Politics, Economics, and the History of Ideas*. Routledge & Kegan Paul.

Hendershott, P. H., & Kane, E. J., 1992. *U.S. Office Market Values during the Past Decade: How Distorted Have Appraisals Been?* Real Estate Economics, 20 (2), 188–206.

Homer, S., & Sylla, R., 2005. *A History of Interest Rates* (4th Edition). Oxford University Press.

James, H., 1996. *International Monetary Cooperation since Bretton Woods*. Oxford University Press.

Joskow, P. L., 1988. Asset Specificity and the Structure of Vertical Relationships: Empirical Evidence. Journal of Law, Economics and Organisation. Reprinted in Williamson, O. E. & Winter, S. G. (eds), 1991. *The Nature of the Firm: Origins. Evolution and Development*. Oxford University Press.

Keynes, J. M., 1923. *A Tract on Monetary Reform*. Macmillan.

Keynes, J. M., 1930. *A Treatise on Money* (Vol. II). The Applied Theory of Money. Macmillan.

Keynes, J. M., 1936. *The General Theory of Employment, Interest and Money*. Macmillan.

Klein, B., 1988. Vertical Integration as Organisational Ownership: the Fisher Body General Motors Relationship Revisited. Reprinted in Williamson, O. E. & Winter, S. G. (eds), 1991. *The Nature of the Firm: Origins, Evolution and Development*. Oxford University Press.

Lamont, O., & Stein, J. C., 1999. *Leverage and House Price Dynamics in U.S. Cities*. RAND Journal of Economics, 30 (3), 498–514.

Laubach, T., & Williams, J. C., 2003. *Measuring the Natural Rate of Interest*. Review of Economics and Statistics, 85 (4), 1063–1070.

Lee, Y. H., 2018. *Vertical Integration and Technological Innovation*. Taylor and Francis.

Macaulay, F. R., 1938. *Some Theoretical Problems Suggested by the Movements of Interest Rates, Bond Yields, and Stock Prices in the United States since 1856*. NBER.

Mankiw, N. G., 2021. *Macroeconomics* (11th Edition). Worth Publishers.

Masten, S. E., 1988. A Legal Basis for the Firm, Journal of Law, Economics and Organisation. Reprinted in Williamson, O. E. & Winter, S. G. (eds), 1991. *The Nature of the Firm: Origins, Evolution and Development*. Oxford University Press.

Meltzer, A. H., 2005. *A History of the Federal Reserve* (Vol. 2): 1951–1986. University of Chicago Press.

Mill, J. S., 1848. *Principles of Political Economy*. John W. Parker.

Mishkin, F. S., 2018. *The Economics of Money, Banking, and Financial Markets* (12th Edition). Pearson.

Peng, L., Tam, P., & Yiu, C. Y., 2008. *The Impact of Interest Rate upon Asset Prices: Evidence from Hong Kong's Property Market*. International Real Estate Review, 11 (2), 131–150.

Piketty, T., 2014. *Capital in the Twenty-First Century. Translated by Arthur Goldhammer*. Harvard University Press.

Porter, G., & Livesay, H. C., 1971. *Merchants and Manufacturers: Studies in the Changing Structure of Nineteenth Century Marketing*. Johns Hopkins Press.
Ramsey, J. B., 1969. *Tests for Specification Errors in Classical Linear Least Squares Regression Analysis*. Journal of the Royal Statistical Society, Series B, 31, 350–371.
Ricardo, D., 1817. *On the Principles of Political Economy and Taxation*. John Murray.
Rogoff, K., 2017. *Dealing with Monetary Paralysis at the Zero Bound*. Journal of Economic Perspectives, 31 (3), 47–66.
Roper, A., 2018. *Vertical Disintegration in the Corporate Hotel Industry*. Taylor and Francis.
Shiller, R. J., 1991. *Arithmetic Repeat Sales Price Estimators*. Journal of Housing Economics, 1 (1), 110–126.
Shiller, R. J., 2003. *From Efficient Markets Theory to Behavioral Finance*. Journal of Economic Perspectives, 17 (1), 83–104.
Shiller, R. J., 2007. *Understanding Recent Trends in House Prices*. Project Syndicate.
Sims, C. A., 1980. *Macroeconomics and Reality*. Econometrica, 48 (1), 1–48.
Sims, C. A., 1992. *Interpreting the Macroeconomic Time Series Facts: The Effects of Monetary Policy*. European Economic Review, 36 (5), 975–1000.
Smith, A., 1776. *An Inquiry into the Nature and Causes of the Wealth of Nations*. W. Strahan and T. Cadell.
Smith, G. D., 1988. *From Monopoly to Competition. The Transformation of Alcoa*. 1888–1986. Cambridge University Press.
Stigler, G. J., 1968. *The Organisation of Industry. Richard D. Irwin, as Quoted.* In Williamson, O. E. (ed), 1975. Markets and Hierarchies. The Free Press.
Stigler, G. J., 1971. *The Theory of Economic Regulation*. Bell Journal of Economics, 2, 3–21.
Taylor, J. B., 1993. *Discretion versus Policy Rules in Practice*. Carnegie-Rochester Conference Series on Public Policy, 39, 195–214.
Tindall, G. B., & Shi, D. E., 1993. *America*. W. W. Norton & Company.
Underwood, J., 1989. *The Will to Win: John Egan and Jaguar*. W H Allen.
Vasicek, O., 1977. *An Equilibrium Characterization of the Term Structure*. Journal of Financial Economics, 5 (2), 177–188.
Wicksell, K., 1898. *Interest and Prices*. Macmillan.
Williamson, O. E., 1971. *The Vertical Integration of Production: Market Failure Considerations*. American Economic Review, 61 (2), 112–123.
Williamson, O. E., 1975. *Markets and Hierarchies*. The Free Press.
Williamson, O. E., 1985. *The Economic Institutions of Capitalism*. The Free Press.

Index

Note: Page references in *italics* denote figures/graph, in **bold** tables and with "n" endnotes.

For Product Safety Concerns and Information please contact our EU representative GPSR@taylorandfrancis.com Taylor & Francis Verlag GmbH, Kaufingerstraße 24, 80331 München, Germany